HOW TO
FENG SHUI
YOUR HOME

HOW TO
FENG SHUI
YOUR HOME

GILL HALE

LORENZ BOOKS

This edition published in 2000 by Lorenz Books

Lorenz Books is an imprint of
Anness Publishing Limited
Hermes House, 88-89 Blackfriars Road
London SE1 8HA

Published in the USA by Lorenz Books
Anness Publishing Inc., 27 West 20th Street, New York, NY 10011; (800) 354-9657

A CIP catalogue record for this book is available from the British Library

Publisher: Joanna Lorenz
Senior Editor: Joanne Rippin
Designer: Nigel Partridge
Special photography: John Freeman
Stylist: Clare Hunt
Illustrator: Geoff Ball
Production Controller: Don Campaniello
Editorial Reader: Richard McGinlay
(for picture acknowledgements see page 126)

Also published as *The Essential Book of Feng Shui: A Complete Guide to Harmonious Modern Living* and
as part of a larger compendium, *The Practical Encyclopedia of Feng Shui*
Updated © 2001
Printed and bound in China

1 3 5 7 9 10 8 6 4 2

CONTENTS

INTRODUCTION

Feng Shui is basically an environmental science and its origins are simple. It is based on an interpretation of the natural world which enabled the Chinese to create efficient agricultural systems, and also the study of the movement of heavenly bodies in order to determine the passage of time. Over the centuries, the interpretation grew more complex and became removed from its original purpose. As its exponents spread out from China across the world, their beliefs altered to fit into local beliefs and customs and, inevitably, folklore and superstition grew up

around them. Fortunately, the ancient Chinese preserved the information in written form. In

essence, all societies retain the knowledge contained in Feng Shui, but it has become absorbed into different disciplines. In China it underlies all aspects of life, from nutrition and medicine to exercise and the arts. By understanding the basic concepts, we can choose designs, meaningful images and symbols from our own culture to support us in our lives.

As practised today, Feng Shui gives us advice on how to create environments in which we feel comfortable and supported. Some of these environments are common sense. Others may not make sense until we understand that by recognizing problem areas in our lives and taking positive steps to improve them, we can connect to the energy of the spaces around us and bring about desired changes.

There is currently much discussion about which is the correct way to practise Feng Shui in the West. Should we stick strictly to what is now called Traditional Chinese Feng Shui or should we allow for other interpretations? Is Feng Shui Chinese, or have we in the West adopted a term which means something else for us? This book aims to set what we have come to understand as Feng

Shui in context and, by using modern examples alongside ancient ones, explore what the basic principles are.

Modern lifestyles leave us little time to stop and consider the effect our surroundings have on us. There is increasing awareness that some aspects of modern technology, the materials we use and the substances we release into the atmosphere can create lasting damage to our health and to the planet. Although this is not Feng Shui in its purest form, concern for our environment and an awareness of the damage we inflict on it must form part of Feng Shui for the present age. We have reached a stage where the human race has become capable of the most amazing feats on the one hand and the most amazing follies on the other. We have the capacity to cure hereditary diseases but also to let genetically-engineered organisms loose into the environment in the most dangerous form of warfare humankind has ever known. We send people into space to collect information never dreamed of half a century ago, yet at the same time we allow the planet we inhabit to become increasingly polluted and less able to sustain the life forms on which we depend for our survival.

These anomalies of modern living are becoming increasingly destructive and more and more people are turning to different approaches to living, in order to attempt to redress the balance. Feng Shui offers us the opportunity to achieve health, happiness and well-being through living in harmony with our environment.

The intention of this book is to interpret Feng Shui for modern times without straying from the underlying principles. While it cannot teach the interpretive skills and understanding which come with many years of study and practice, it is possible to give an insight into how we can interpret the principles to create nurturing and life-enhancing supportive spaces in our homes. This knowledge will enable us to make an impact on the wider environment so that we can preserve it for future generations.

WHAT IS FENG SHUI?

The Chinese have a saying, "First, luck; second, destiny; third, Feng Shui; fourth, virtues; fifth, education": although Feng Shui can be a powerful force in shaping our lives, it is not a cure for all ills. Luck plays a major role, and personality, or karma, is almost as important. What we do with our lives and how we behave towards others will play a part, and education gives us the tools to make sense of the world. Feng Shui is just one part of the complete package.

▲ *In China the dragon symbolizes good fortune. Its presence is felt in landforms and watercourses.*

▲ *The Dragon Hills which protect Hong Kong are believed to be responsible for its prosperity.*

The single factor which sets Feng Shui apart from other philosophical systems is that it has the capacity for change built into it. Most systems evolved from similar principles; understanding the natural world played a major role and natural phenomena were believed to be imbued with a spirit or deity, recognition of which would give people some benefit in their lives. Where these systems became established as religions, the deities were worshipped, but Feng Shui has remained a philosophy and can be used in any culture and alongside any belief system.

▶ *Much of the symbolic imagery in Feng Shui is taken from landscapes such as this in Guilin, southern China.*

Feng Shui uses formulae which determine the rising and falling energy in a given time span of an individual or a house. Other formulae indicate a person's best location within a home or office, and can suggest the best placing of beds and desks. Many Chinese people consult astrologers annually to further refine this, so that every activity within the year can be pinpointed accurately and undertaken at an auspicious time. This can be as precise as the best time to conceive or even when to wash your hair.

The philosophy of Feng Shui is embraced by people who are aware of the impact their surroundings have on them and feel the need to take action to improve their lives, but using Feng Shui correctly is a skill and its principles cannot be adapted simply to suit the circumstances of a place or an individual.

▼ *Our surroundings affect us. Fresh air, natural products and a healthy environment enhance our mental and physical well-being.*

Feng Shui enables us to position ourselves within our environment to our best advantage. The positioning of our houses and offices as well as their internal design affects each of us positively or negatively. Feng Shui helps us to determine the most favourable positions for us and the layouts, colours and designs which will support us. In the garden we can determine the best locations for the different activities we intend to pursue there, but we also have to take account of the plants in the garden and their needs, which are equally important if the environment is to thrive.

▲ *Water energy plays a significant role in Feng Shui. Here a fountain brings life to an office courtyard.*

The following chapters provide information on those aspects of this complex and fascinating subject that can be utilized by everyone in their own space. When we introduce Feng Shui into our lives we can only benefit, even where we only touch the surface. As we become more aware of our surroundings, and actively begin to change those factors with which we feel uncomfortable, we begin to gain a deeper insight into ourselves and our part in the wider picture.

▼ *The T'ung Shui almanac, produced for centuries, details the best times to move house, conceive and even wash your hair.*

APPROACHES TO FENG SHUI

Feng Shui is about interpreting environments. Practitioners use a number of different approaches to connect with the energy or "feel" of a place, and fine-tune it to make it work for those living or working there. Provided the principles are understood, the different approaches will be effective. More often than not, practitioners use a mixture of methods to create the effects they want.

THE ENVIRONMENTAL APPROACH

In ancient times, people lived by their wits and knowledge of local conditions. Their needs were basic: food and shelter. Observation would tell them from which direction the prevailing winds were coming and they would build their homes in protective sites. They needed water in order to grow and transport their crops so rivers were important, and the direction of the flow and the orientation of the banks would determine the type of crops which could be grown. This branch of Feng Shui is known as the Form or Landform School and was the earliest approach to the subject.

▼ *The Form School regards this as the ideal spot on which to build. The Black Tortoise hill at the rear offers support while the White Tiger and Green Dragon give protection from the wind, with the all-powerful dragon slightly higher than the Tiger. The Red Phoenix marks the front boundary, and the river irrigates the site and enables crops to be transported for trade.*

BLACK TORTOISE

WHITE TIGER

GREEN DRAGON

RED PHOENIX

▲ *These "Karst" limestone hills in China symbolically protect an area of rich agricultural land.*

▶ *A luo pan or compass, used by geomancers in ancient China. Much of the information it records is regularly used by Feng Shui consultants.*

THE COMPASS APPROACH

In ancient China, geomancers investigated earth formations and watercourses while astronomers charted the skies. Those who understood the power of the information they possessed recorded their knowledge on an instrument called a luo pan, or compass. The luo pan not only illustrates direction, but also investigates the energy of each direction, depending on the landform or heavenly body to be found there. Interpreting these energies suggests suitable sites for human beings. Feng Shui is based on the *I Ching*, a philosophical book which interprets the energies of the universe. Its 64 images from the yearly nature cycle form the outer ring of the luo pan. With the wisdom of ancient sages added to it over the centuries, the *I Ching* offers us a means to connect to the natural flow of the universe. Its built-in time factor allows individuals to connect to it in different ways at different times in their lives.

THE INTUITIVE APPROACH

Ancient texts illustrate every shape of mountain and watercourse. The names illustrate concepts significant to the Chinese psyche. "Tiger in Waiting" suggests a negative place, where residents will never be able to relax, whereas "Baby Dragon Looking at its Mother" indicates a much more restful environment.

The ancient text of the *Water Dragon Classic* provides more information on the best places to build, showing flow direction and position within the tributaries, with the names again indicating the type of environment. The sensibilities of people living and working on the land were finely tuned and their knowledge of the natural world endowed them with an instinct for suitable sites to grow crops.

▶ *Mountain sites (1 & 2) and river sites (3 & 4); the dots represent buildings. All except for "Tiger in Waiting" are auspicious positions to build a new home.*

▼ *This prime site is protected by mountains, with healthy watercourses.*

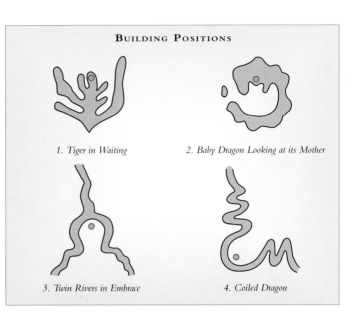

BUILDING POSITIONS

1. Tiger in Waiting

2. Baby Dragon Looking at its Mother

3. Twin Rivers in Embrace

4. Coiled Dragon

THE PRINCIPLES OF FENG SHUI

Ancient peoples regarded the heavens, the earth and themselves as part of one system. This holistic view of life persists in many cultures, where health and medicine, food and lifestyle, and the route to salvation are all interconnected in one ecological system.

THE WAY

The Tao, or the Way, the philosophy of which underlies Feng Shui, shows how to order our lives to live in harmony with ourselves, each other and the natural world. We can use Feng Shui to help us work towards achieving this.

▼ *"The Dragon Breathing on the Lake" – the lake is a powerful Chinese image, symbolizing a light-reflective surface harbouring a dark and deep interior.*

YIN AND YANG

Positive and negative forces act together in order to create energy – in electricity, for instance. Yin and yang represent these two forces which are in constant movement, each attempting to gain dominance. Where one achieves dominance, an imbalance occurs, so when one

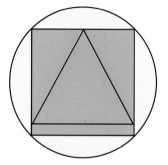

force becomes too strong its influence subsides and the other takes over. Still water, for example, is yin; a raging torrent is yang. Imagine a slow-moving yin river. When it hits rocks and descends, turbulence occurs, it speeds up and becomes yang. When it flows into a lake, it slows down and becomes yin once more. Yin and yang are opposing but interdependent concepts – without the idea of cold we would not be able to describe heat. At their extremes they

▲ *The T'ai Chi symbol illustrates the concept of yin and yang, the opposite yet interdependent forces that drive the world.*

◀ *Circle, Square, Triangle – signifying Heaven, Earth, human beings – the universal cosmological symbol.*

Yin	**Yang**
Moon	Sun
Winter	Summer
Dark	Light
Feminine	Masculine
Interior	Exterior
Low	High
Stillness	Movement
Passive	Active
Odd numbers	Even numbers
Earth	Heaven
Cold	Heat
Soft	Hard
Valleys	Hills
Still water	Mountains
Gardens	Houses
Sleep	Wakefulness

change into each other; ice can burn and sunstroke sufferers shiver. The aim is to achieve a balance between them. There are examples throughout the book of how we can achieve this in our own environments. Some of the more common associations are listed left.

CHI

Chi is a concept unknown in Western philosophy but figures repeatedly in the philosophies of the East. It is the life force of all animate things, the quality of environments, the power of the sun, the moon and weather systems, and the driving force in human beings. In China, the movements in T'ai Chi encourage chi to move through the body. Acupuncture needles are used to unblock its flow when stuck. Chinese herbal medicine uses the special energetic qualities of herbs to correct chi when it becomes unbalanced. Meditation helps to establish a healthy mind: every brush stroke of the Chinese artist or sweep of the calligrapher's pen is the result of trained mental processes and the correct breathing

▼ *An acupuncturist at work. The needles unblock the energy channels and enable chi to flow round the body.*

▲ *Chinese people practising T'ai Chi. The exercises are designed to aid the flow of chi in the body.*

techniques, which ensure that each carefully composed painting or document is infused with chi.

The purpose of Feng Shui is to create environments in which chi flows smoothly to achieve physical and mental health. Where chi flows gently through a house, the occupants will be positive and will have an easy passage through life. Where chi moves sluggishly or becomes stuck, then the chances are that problems will occur in the day-to-day life or long-term prospects of those living there.

Where chi flows smoothly in the garden, the plants will be healthy and the wildlife there will flourish. Animals, birds, insects and the myriad of unseen micro-organisms that live there will regulate themselves and create a balanced and supportive environment. Where chi cannot flow unimpeded and becomes sluggish or stuck, an area may become dank or there may be an imbalance which creates, say, a plague of aphids.

In an office where chi flows freely, employees will be happy and supportive, projects will be completed on time and stress levels will be low. Where the chi is stuck, there will be disharmony and the business will not flourish.

FIVE TYPES OF ENERGY

Some of the latest scientific theories enable us to make sense of the ancient formulae on which Feng Shui is based. It is accepted that everything in the universe vibrates. All our senses and everything we encounter are attuned to certain frequencies, which react with us in a positive or negative way. We are all familiar with sound waves, which bring us radio, and electromagnetic waves, which bring us television. Colours, shapes, food, weather conditions – everything in our lives affects us on a vibrational level for good or ill and, in turn, we react in various yet predictable ways, depending on our individual traits.

The concept of elements exists throughout the world. The Chinese recognize five which arise out of the interplay of yin and yang and represent different manifestations of chi. They represent a classification system for everything in the universe, including people, some of these are shown in the "Relationships of the Five Elements" table.

Ideally, there should be a balance of all the elements. Where one dominates or is lacking, then difficulties occur. Interpreting and balancing the elements plays a major part in the practice of Feng Shui. The elements move in a predetermined way, illustrated as a cycle in which they all support each other. A useful way of remembering this is by looking at the cycle in the following way. Water enables Wood to grow, Wood enables Fire to burn resulting in ashes or Earth, in which forms Metal, which in liquid form resembles Water. Another cycle indicates how the elements control each other and can be memorized as follows: Water extinguishes Fire, and in turn is soaked up by the Earth, which is depleted of energy by Wood in the form of trees, which can be destroyed by Metal tools. the "Relationships of the Five Elements" table introduces another aspect – how in supporting another element, an element can itself be weakened. The applications of the five elements are illustrated throughout this book.

▲ *Storms are nature's way of restoring a balance. They replenish negative ions in the atmosphere, which improves air quality.*

▼ *The heavenly bodies are essential to our lives and their movements lie at the heart of Feng Shui.*

THE RELATIONSHIPS OF THE FIVE ELEMENTS				
ELEMENT	HELPED BY	HARMED BY	WEAKENED BY	WEAKENS
Wood	Water	Metal	Fire	Earth
Fire	Wood	Water	Earth	Metal
Earth	Fire	Wood	Metal	Water
Metal	Earth	Fire	Water	Wood
Water	Metal	Earth	Wood	Fire

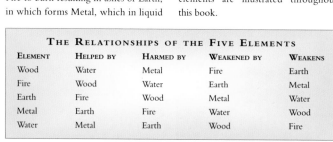

THE FIVE ELEMENTS

ELEMENT	CHARACTERISTICS	PERSONALITIES	ASSOCIATIONS
WOOD	Symbolizes spring, growth and plant life. In its yin form, it is supple and pliable, in its yang form as sturdy as an oak. Positively used, it is a walking stick; negatively used, a spear. Bamboo is cherished in China for its ability to sway in the wind yet be used as scaffolding. Viewed as a tree, Wood energy is expansive, nurturing and versatile.	Wood people are public-spirited and energetic. Ideas people, their outgoing personalities win them support. They visualize rather than committing themselves to plans. *Positively* – they are artistic and undertake tasks with enthusiasm. *Negatively* – they become impatient and angry and often fail to finish the tasks they have begun.	Trees and plants Wooden furniture Paper Green Columns Decking Landscape pictures
FIRE	Symbolizes summer, fire and heat. It can bring light, warmth and happiness or it can erupt, explode and destroy with great violence. Positively, it stands for honour and fairness. Negatively, it stands for aggression and war.	Fire people are leaders and crave action. They inspire others to follow, often into trouble, as they dislike rules and fail to see consequences. *Positively* – they are innovative, humorous and passionate people. *Negatively* – they are impatient, exploit others and have little thought for their feelings.	Sun symbols Candles, lights and lamps Triangles Red Man-made materials Sun or fire pictures
EARTH	Symbolizes the nurturing environment that enables seeds to grow, which all living things emanate from and return to. It nurtures, supports and interacts with each of the other elements. Positively, it denotes fairness, wisdom and instinct. Negatively, it can smother or represent the nervous anticipation of non-existent problems.	Earth people are supportive and loyal. Practical and persevering, they are a tower of strength in a crisis. They do not rush anything, but their support is enduring. Patient and steady, they possess inner strength. *Positively* – earth people are loyal, dependable and patient. *Negatively* – they are obsessional and prone to nit-picking.	Clay, brick and terracotta Cement and stone Squares Yellow, orange and brown
METAL	Symbolizes autumn and strength. Its nature represents solidity and the ability to contain objects. On the other hand, metal is also a conductor. Positively, it represents communication, brilliant ideas and justice. Negatively, it can suggest destruction, danger and sadness. Metal can be a beautiful and precious commodity, or the blade of a weapon.	Metal people are dogmatic and resolute. They pursue their ambitious aims single-mindedly. Good organizers, they are independent and happy in their own company. Faith in their own abilities inclines them towards inflexibility although they thrive on change. They are serious and do not accept help easily. *Positively* – they are strong, intuitive and interesting people. *Negatively* – they are inflexible, melancholic and serious.	All metals Round shapes Domes Metal objects Door furniture and doorsteps Kitchenware White, grey, silver and gold Coins Clocks
WATER	Symbolizes winter and water itself, gentle rain or a storm. It suggests the inner self, art and beauty. It touches everything. Positively, it nurtures and supports with understanding. Negatively, it can wear down and exhaust. Associated with the emotions, it can suggest fear, nervousness and stress.	Water people communicate well. They are diplomatic and persuasive. Sensitive to the moods of others, they will lend an ear. They are intuitive and make excellent negotiators. Flexible and adaptable, they view things holistically. *Positively* – water people are artistic, sociable and sympathetic. *Negatively* – water people are sensitive, fickle and intrusive.	Rivers, streams and lakes Blue and black Mirrors and glass Meandering patterns Fountains and ponds Fish tanks Water pictures

CHINESE ASTROLOGY

An analysis of an environment using a luo pan compass looks at the energetic qualities of the various compass points. The Earthly Branches on the compass represent 12 of these points and also correspond to the 12 animals which relate to Chinese astrology. We often find ourselves in situations at home, or at work, when we canot understand how another person can view the same situation so differently from us, or can make us feel uncomfortable, or find different things irritating or amusing. Looking at the animals enables us to explore these differences by allowing us an insight into the make-up of our natures and personalities.

With this knowledge, we can come to know ourselves better and to accept the personalities of others. At home, it may encourage us to think twice, for instance, before launching into a tirade on tidiness or punctuality. It also has an important use in the workplace in keeping warring factions apart and ensuring a harmonious balance between productive output and socializing.

THE CYCLES

The Chinese calendar is based on the cycle of the moon, which determines that each month is approximately 29½ days long, beginning with a new moon. The years progress in cycles of 12 and it is helpful to appreciate the subtleties of Chinese symbology since each year is represented by an animal and the characteristics of each animal and its way of life are used to identify different types of people. Cultural differences are apt to get in the way if we attempt this identification ourselves; whereas Westerners would describe the Rat's character, for example, as sly and crafty, the Chinese respect its quick mind and native cunning.

◀ In the Chinese calendar each year is represented by an animal and each animal is governed by an element.

Each animal is governed by an element which determines its intrinsic nature. The cycle of 12 is repeated five times to form a larger cycle of 60 years and in each of these cycles, the animals are ascribed an element with either a yin or yang characteristic, which determines their characters. Thus in 60 years, no two animals are the same. We begin by investigating the basic animal characteristics.

THE NATURE OF THE ANIMALS

Rat	Water
Ox	Earth
Tiger	Wood
Rabbit	Wood
Dragon	Earth
Snake	Fire
Horse	Fire
Goat	Earth
Monkey	Metal
Rooster	Metal
Dog	Earth
Pig	Water

If we do not get on with someone, it may be that the animals associated with us in the Chinese calendar are not compatible. Alternatively, it may be that the elements that represent the time of our birth are not in harmony with the elements of the other person.

FINDING YOUR ANIMAL

The Chinese year does not begin on 1st January but on a date which corresponds with the second new moon after the winter equinox, so it varies from year to year. Thus someone born on 25th January 1960 according to the Western calendar would actually be born in 1959 according to the Chinese calendar. The "Chinese Animals Table" opposite gives the exact dates when each year begins and ends, as well as its ruling animal and element. Their outer characteristics are identified by the element of the year they were born, as shown in "The Nature of the Animals" box (left). The ways in which the elements affect an animal's personality are described in "The Five Elements" table.

ANIMAL CYCLES

One of the 12 animals represents each lunar month, each with its own element governing its intrinsic nature. Over 60 years, the Five Elements cycle spins so that each animal can be Wood, Fire, Earth, Metal or Water, which determines its character.

In a full analysis by an experienced Feng Shui consultant, each of us will have a collection of eight elements that together make up not only our character, but also our destiny.

CHINESE ANIMALS TABLE

Year	Year Begins	Year Ends	Animal	Element	Year	Year Begins	Year Ends	Animal	Element
1920	20 February 1920	7 February 1921	Monkey	Metal +	1967	9 February 1967	29 January 1968	Goat	Fire −
1921	8 February 1921	27 January 1922	Rooster	Metal −	1968	30 January 1968	16 February 1969	Monkey	Earth +
1922	28 January 1922	15 February 1923	Dog	Water +	1969	17 February 1969	5 February 1970	Rooster	Earth −
1923	16 February 1923	4 February 1924	Pig	Water −	1970	6 February 1970	26 January 1971	Dog	Metal +
1924	5 February 1924	24 January 1925	Rat	Wood +	1971	27 January 1971	15 February 1972	Pig	Metal −
1925	25 January 1925	12 February 1926	Ox	Wood −	1972	16 February 1972	2 February 1973	Rat	Water +
1926	13 February 1926	1 February 1927	Tiger	Fire +	1973	3 February 1973	22 January 1974	Ox	Water −
1927	2 February 1927	22 January 1928	Rabbit	Fire −	1974	23 January 1974	10 February 1975	Tiger	Wood +
1928	23 January 1928	9 February 1929	Dragon	Earth +	1975	11 February 1975	30 January 1976	Rabbit	Wood −
1929	10 February 1929	29 January 1930	Snake	Earth −	1976	31 January 1976	17 February 1977	Dragon	Fire +
1930	30 January 1930	16 February 1931	Horse	Metal +	1977	18 February 1977	6 February 1978	Snake	Fire −
1931	17 February 1931	5 February 1932	Goat	Metal −	1978	7 February 1978	27 January 1979	Horse	Earth +
1932	6 February 1932	25 January 1933	Monkey	Water +	1979	28 January 1979	15 February 1980	Goat	Earth −
1933	26 January 1933	13 February 1934	Rooster	Water −	1980	16 February 1980	4 February 1981	Monkey	Metal +
1934	14 February 1934	3 February 1935	Dog	Wood +	1981	5 February 1981	24 January 1982	Rooster	Metal −
1935	4 February 1935	23 January 1936	Pig	Wood −	1982	25 January 1982	12 February 1983	Dog	Water +
1936	24 January 1936	10 February 1937	Rat	Fire +	1983	13 February 1983	1 February 1984	Pig	Water −
1937	11 February 1937	30 January 1938	Ox	Fire −	1984	2 February 1984	19 February 1985	Rat	Wood +
1938	31 January 1938	18 February 1939	Tiger	Earth +	1985	20 February 1985	8 February 1986	Ox	Wood −
1939	19 February 1939	7 February 1940	Rabbit	Earth −	1986	9 February 1986	28 January 1987	Tiger	Fire +
1940	8 February 1940	26 January 1941	Dragon	Metal +	1987	29 January 1987	16 February 1988	Rabbit	Fire −
1941	27 January 1941	14 February 1942	Snake	Metal −	1988	17 February 1988	5 February 1989	Dragon	Earth +
1942	15 February 1942	4 February 1943	Horse	Water +	1989	6 February 1989	26 January 1990	Snake	Earth −
1943	5 February 1943	24 January 1944	Goat	Water −	1990	27 January 1990	14 February 1991	Horse	Metal +
1944	25 January 1944	12 February 1945	Monkey	Wood +	1991	15 February 1991	3 February 1992	Goat	Metal −
1945	13 February 1945	1 February 1946	Rooster	Wood −	1992	4 February 1992	22 January 1993	Monkey	Water +
1946	2 February 1946	21 January 1947	Dog	Fire +	1993	23 January 1993	9 February 1994	Rooster	Water −
1947	22 January 1947	9 February 1948	Pig	Fire −	1994	10 February 1994	30 January 1995	Dog	Wood +
1948	10 February 1948	28 January 1949	Rat	Earth +	1995	31 January 1995	18 February 1996	Pig	Wood −
1949	29 January 1949	16 February 1950	Ox	Earth −	1996	19 February 1996	6 February 1997	Rat	Fire +
1950	17 February 1950	5 February 1951	Tiger	Metal +	1997	7 February 1997	27 January 1998	Ox	Fire −
1951	6 February 1951	26 January 1952	Rabbit	Metal −	1998	28 January 1998	15 February 1999	Tiger	Earth +
1952	27 January 1952	13 February 1953	Dragon	Water +	1999	16 February 1999	4 February 2000	Rabbit	Earth −
1953	14 February 1953	2 February 1954	Snake	Water −	2000	5 February 2000	23 January 2001	Dragon	Metal +
1954	3 February 1954	23 January 1955	Horse	Wood +	2001	24 January 2001	11 February 2002	Snake	Metal −
1955	24 January 1955	11 February 1956	Goat	Wood −	2002	12 February 2002	31 January 2003	Horse	Water +
1956	12 February 1956	30 January 1957	Monkey	Fire +	2003	1 February 2003	21 January 2004	Goat	Water −
1957	31 January 1957	17 February 1958	Rooster	Fire −	2004	22 January 2004	8 February 2005	Monkey	Wood +
1958	18 February 1958	7 February 1959	Dog	Earth +	2005	9 February 2005	28 January 2006	Rooster	Wood −
1959	8 February 1959	27 January 1960	Pig	Earth −	2006	29 January 2006	17 February 2007	Dog	Fire +
1960	28 January 1960	14 February 1961	Rat	Metal +	2007	18 February 2007	6 February 2008	Pig	Fire −
1961	15 February 1961	4 February 1962	Ox	Metal −	2008	7 February 2008	25 January 2009	Rat	Earth +
1962	5 February 1962	24 January 1963	Tiger	Water +	2009	26 January 2009	13 February 2010	Ox	Earth −
1963	25 January 1963	12 February 1964	Rabbit	Water −	2010	14 February 2010	2 February 2011	Tiger	Metal +
1964	13 February 1964	1 February 1965	Dragon	Wood +	2011	3 February 2011	22 January 2012	Rabbit	Metal −
1965	2 February 1965	20 January 1966	Snake	Wood −	2012	23 January 2012	9 February 2013	Dragon	Water +
1966	21 January 1966	8 February 1967	Horse	Fire +	2013	10 February 2013	30 January 2014	Snake	Water −

THE ANIMAL SIGNS

Using characteristics that are perceived to be an inherent part of the natures of the 12 animals, Chinese astrology attributes certain aspects of these to the characteristics and behaviour of people born at specific times. This system operates in much the same way as Western astrology.

THE RAT

The Rat is an opportunist with an eye for a bargain. Rats tend to collect and hoard, but are unwilling to pay too much for anything. They are devoted to their families, particularly their children. On the surface, Rats are sociable and gregarious yet underneath they can be miserly and petty. Quick-witted and passionate, they are capable of deep emotions despite their cool exteriors. Their nervous energy and ambition may lead Rats to attempt more tasks than they are able to complete successfully. Rats will stand by their friends as long as they receive their support in return. However, they are not above using information given to them in confidence in order to advance their own cause.

▼ *Sociable and family-minded, rats are quick witted and opportunistic.*

▼ *Dependable and loyal, the Ox displays endless patience until pushed too far.*

THE OX

The Ox is solid and dependable. Oxen are excellent organizers and systematic in their approach to every task they undertake. They are not easily influenced by others' ideas. Loyalty is part of their make-up, but if crossed or deceived they will never forget. Oxen do not appear to be imaginative though they are capable of good ideas. Although not demonstrative or the most exciting people romantically, they are entirely dependable

▲ *Dynamic and generous, Tigers are warm-hearted unless they are crossed.*

and make devoted parents. They are people of few words but fine understated gestures. Oxen are renowned for their patience, but it has its limits – once roused, their temper is a sight to behold.

THE TIGER

The Tiger is dynamic, impulsive and lives life to the full. Tigers often leap into projects without planning, but their natural exuberance will carry them through successfully unless boredom creeps in and they do not complete the task. Tigers do not like failure and need to be admired. If their spirits fall, they require a patient ear to listen until they bounce back again. They like excitement in their relationships and static situations leave them cold. Tigers are egotistic. They can be generous and warm, but will also sometimes show their claws.

THE RABBIT

The Rabbit is a born diplomat and cannot bear conflict. Rabbits can be evasive and will often give the answer they think someone wishes to hear rather than enter into a discussion. This is not to say they give in easily: the docile cover hides a strong will and self-assurance. It is difficult to gauge what Rabbits are thinking and they can often appear to be constantly daydreaming, though in reality they may be planning their next strategy. The calmest of the animal signs, Rabbits are social creatures up to the point when their space is invaded. Good communication skills enable Rabbits to enjoy the company of others and they are good counsellors. They prefer to keep away from the limelight where possible and to enjoy the finer things of life.

▲ *Good counsellors and communicators, Rabbits also need their own space.*

THE DRAGON

The Dragon will launch straight into projects or conversations with a pioneering spirit. Dragons often fail to notice others trying to keep up or indeed those plotting behind their backs. Authority figures, they make their own laws and cannot bear restriction. They prefer to get on with a job themselves and are good at motivating others into action.

▲ *Powerful leaders, Dragons prefer to follow their own path in life.*

They are always available to help others, but their pride makes it difficult for them to accept help in return. Although they are always at the centre of things, they tend to be loners and are prone to stress when life becomes difficult. Hard-working and generous, Dragons are entirely trustworthy and are loyal friends. They enjoy excitement and new situations. When upset, they can be explosive, but all is soon forgotten.

THE SNAKE

The Snake is a connoisseur of the good things in life. Inward-looking and self-reliant, Snakes tend to keep their own counsel and dislike relying on others. They can be ruthless in pursuing their goals. Although very kind and generous, Snakes can be demanding in relationships. They find it hard to forgive and will never forget a slight. Never underestimate the patience of a snake, who will wait in the wings until the time is right to strike. They are elegant and sophisticated and although they are good at making money, they never spend it on trifles. Only the best is good enough for them. Very intuitive, Snakes can sense the motives of others and can sum up situations accurately. If crossed, Snakes will bite back with deadly accuracy. They exude an air of mystery, ooze charm and can be deeply passionate.

▼ *Mysterious and passionate, Snakes have endless patience.*

▲ *Active and excitable, the Horse's nervous energy often runs away with them.*

THE HORSE

The Horse is ever-active. Horses will work tirelessly until a project is completed, but only if the deadline is their own. Horses have lightning minds and can sum up people and situations in an instant, sometimes too quickly, and they will move on before seeing the whole picture. Capable of undertaking several tasks at once, Horses are constantly on the move and fond of exercise. They may exhaust themselves physically and mentally. Horses are ambitious and confident in their own abilities. They are not interested in the opinions of others and are adept at side-stepping issues. They can be impatient and have explosive tempers although they rarely bear grudges.

THE GOAT

The Goat is emotional and compassionate. Peace-lovers, Goats always behave correctly and they are extremely accommodating to others. They tend to be shy and vulnerable to criticism. They worry a lot and appear to be easily put upon, but when they feel strongly about something they will dig their heels in and sulk until they achieve their objectives. Goats are generally popular and are usually well cared for by others. They appreciate the finer things in life and are usually lucky. They find it difficult to deal with difficulties and deprivation. Ardent romantics, Goats can obtain their own way by wearing their partners down and turning every occasion to their advantage. They will do anything to avoid conflict and hate making decisions.

▼ *Peace-loving Goats are kind and popular, they hate conflict and will try to avoid it.*

THE MONKEY

The Monkey is intelligent and capable of using its wits to solve problems. Monkeys often wriggle out of difficult situations and are not above trickery if it will further their own ends. Monkeys tend to be oblivious of other people and of the effect their own actions may have on them. In spite of this, they are usually popular and are able to motivate others by their sheer enthusiasm for new projects. Monkeys are constantly on the look out for new challenges and their innovative approach and excellent memories generally make them successful. They are full of energy and are always active. They have little sympathy for those who are unable to keep up with them, but will soon forget any difficulties.

▼ *Energetic Monkeys use their intelligence to push their own ideas forward.*

▲ *The flamboyant Rooster can be easily won over by flattery and admiration.*

THE ROOSTER

The Rooster is a very sociable creature. Roosters shine in situations where they are able to be the centre of attention. If a Rooster is present, everyone will be aware of the fact because no Rooster can ever take a back seat at a social gathering. They are dignified, confident and extremely strong-willed, yet they may have a negative streak. They excel in arguments and debates. Incapable of underhandedness, Roosters lay all their cards on the table and do not spare others' feelings in their quest to do the right thing. They never weary of getting to the bottom of a problem and are perfectionists in all that they do. Roosters can usually be won over by flattery. Full of energy, Roosters are brave, but they hate criticism and can be puritanical in their approach to life.

THE DOG

The Dog is entirely dependable and has an inherent sense of justice. Intelligent, Dogs are loyal to their friends and they always listen to the problems of others, although they can be critical. In a crisis, Dogs will always help and they will never betray a friend. They can be hard workers, but are

▼ *Dogs are loyal and hard-working, but enjoy relaxing too.*

not all that interested in accumulating wealth for themselves. They like to spend time relaxing. Dogs take time to get to know people but have a tendency to pigeon-hole them. When they want something badly they can be persistent. If roused they can be obstinate and occasionally they lash out, although their temper is usually short-lived. Some Dogs can be rather nervous and they may be prone to pessimism.

▲ *Peace-loving Pigs are sociable and popular and are able to organize others well.*

THE PIG

The Pig is everybody's friend. Honest and generous, Pigs are always available to bail others out of difficulties. Pigs love the social scene and are popular. They rarely argue and if they do fly off the handle, they bear no grudges afterwards. They abhor conflict and very often will not notice when others are attempting to upset them. They prefer to think well of people. Overindulgence is their greatest weakness and Pigs will spend heavily in pursuit of pleasure. They always share with their friends and trust that, in return, their friends will make allowances for their own little weaknesses. Great organizers, Pigs like to have a cause and will often rally others to it as well.

COMPATIBILITY OF SIGNS

The saying, "You can choose your friends but not your family", is often heard from those who do not have harmonious family relationships, and we all find that we are drawn more to some people than to others. Chinese astrology uses the year, month, day and time of birth (each of which is represented by an animal and the yin or yang attributes of its accompanying element) to analyse characters and predict fortunes. Analyses of relationships depend upon the interaction of the elements on each person's chart. We can gain some insight into our

▼ *We are drawn to people for a variety of reasons. Compatibility of animal signs and elements can certainly help.*

own characters and those of our family and colleagues by using the "Chinese Animals Table" and then looking at the associated elements with their yang (+) (positive characteristics) or yin (–) (negative characteristics) in "The Five Elements" table.

▲ *We function well at work when we are compatible with our colleagues. The man on the right looks uncomfortable.*

▼ *This table shows which of our family, friends and colleagues we relate to best according to Chinese astrology.*

COMPATIBILITY TABLE

	Rat	Ox	Tiger	Rabbit	Dragon	Snake	Horse	Goat	Monkey	Rooster	Dog	Pig
Rat	+	=	+	–	★	=	–	–	★	–	+	+
Ox	=	+	–	=	+	★	–	–	+	★	+	+
Tiger	+	–	+	–	+	=	★	+	–	=	★	=
Rabbit	+	+	–	+	=	+	–	★	–	–	=	★
Dragon	★	–	+	=	–	+	–	+	★	+	–	+
Snake	+	★	–	+	=	+	+	–	–	★	+	–
Horse	–	–	★	–	=	+	+	=	+	+	★	+
Goat	–	–	=	★	+	+	=	+	+	–	–	★
Monkey	★	+	–	–	★	–	–	+	=	+	+	+
Rooster	–	★	+	–	–	★	+	=	–	+	+	+
Dog	+	–	★	=	–	+	★	–	+	–	=	+
Pig	=	+	=	★	+	–	–	★	–	+	+	+

Key: ★ Excellent = Good + Workable – Difficult

THE ANIMAL YEARS

As we have seen, each year is ruled by an animal and its character is said to denote the energetic quality of the year.

The animal which rules each year and the date of the Chinese New Year for around a hundred-year period are shown on the "Chinese Animals Table". For ease of reference, 1999–2010 are shown below. Our fortunes in each year are indicated by whether or not we are compatible with the animal ruling that year, which can be checked by referring back to the "Compatibility Table".

1999	Rabbit	2005	Rooster
2000	Dragon	2006	Dog
2001	Snake	2007	Pig
2002	Horse	2008	Rat
2003	Goat	2009	Ox
2004	Monkey	2010	Tiger

YEAR OF THE RABBIT
A respite from the past year and a breather before the next, rest is indicated here. This is a time for negotiations and settlements, but not for new ventures. Women's and family concerns are considered important.

YEAR OF THE DRAGON
The time for new business ventures and projects. Euphoric and unpredictable, this is the year for outlandish schemes and taking risks. Dragon babies are considered lucky.

YEAR OF THE SNAKE
Peace returns and allows time to reflect. Care should be taken in business matters as treachery and underhand dealings are indicated. Money is made and communication is good. A fertile year, in which morality becomes an issue.

YEAR OF THE HORSE
An energetic and volatile year in which money will be spent and borrowed. Some impulsive behaviour will bring rewards, while some will fail. A year for marriage and divorce.

YEAR OF THE GOAT
A quiet year in which family matters are to the fore. A year for consolidating and for diplomatic negotiations, rather than launching new projects.

YEAR OF THE MONKEY
An unpredictable year when nothing goes according to plan. Only the quick-witted will prosper. New ideas abound and communication will flourish.

YEAR OF THE ROOSTER
A year for making feelings known and letting grievances out. This may cause disharmony in families so tact is required.

YEAR OF THE DOG
Worthy causes abound – human and animal rights and environmental issues are in the public eye. Security should be

▼ *Family relationships are usually harmonious if the animal signs are compatible and the elements do not clash.*

checked, by governments and at home. A year for marriage and the family.

YEAR OF THE PIG
The last year of the cycle and unfinished business should be concluded. Optimism abounds and the pursuit of leisure is indicated. Family concerns will go well.

YEAR OF THE RAT
This is a lucky year, a good time to start a new venture. The rewards will not come without hard work, but with careful planning they will arrive.

YEAR OF THE OX
Harvest is the symbol for this year so we will reap what we have sown. Decisions should be made now and contracts signed. This is a conservative year so grand or outrageous schemes are not considered appropriate.

YEAR OF THE TIGER
Sudden conflicts and crises arise in this year and will have an impact for some time. The year for grand schemes for the courageous, but underhand activities may suffer from repercussions.

THE BAGUA AND THE MAGIC SQUARE

The compass directions and their associations are fundamental to the practice of Feng Shui. Astronomical and geomantic calculations and the place of human beings within them are plotted on a luo pan, an instrument so powerful that it has been likened to a computer. The luo pan can indicate, to those who know how to interpret it, which illness someone in a certain location might be suffering from, or the fortunes of a person living in a certain room in a house.

This vast amount of information has been reduced to a shorthand form incorporated in a "Magic Square". In cultures worldwide, this was used as a talisman. Many formulae based on the magic square are used to discover whether a place is auspicious, in itself and for the people living there, and the simplest of these are introduced in this book. The diagram on the right shows how the energies repre-sented by the Magic Square always move in a fixed pattern. These patterns are repeat-ed over time and can indicate the fortunes of a person or building in a certain year.

THE BAGUA

The information contained in the luo pan is condensed into the Magic Square, which forms the basis of the Bagua, or Pa Kua, a tool we can use to investigate our homes and offices. The Bagua below holds some of the images which describe the energies of the eight directions and the central position. The Bagua repre-sents the journey of life, the Tao, and we can use it to create comfortable living, working and leisure spaces.

When applying Feng Shui principles to your house, garden or office you will need a tracing of the Bagua with the colours, compass points and directions all added on.

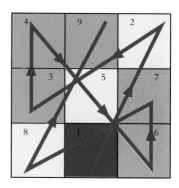

▲ *The Magic Square: the "magic" lies in the fact that every line adds up to 15. Magic squares exist all over the world. In ancient cultures, such symbols were a source of power to their initiates. In Hebrew culture, the pattern formed by the movement of energies is known as the seal of Saturn and is used in Western magic. In Islamic cultures, intricate patterns are based on complex magic squares.*

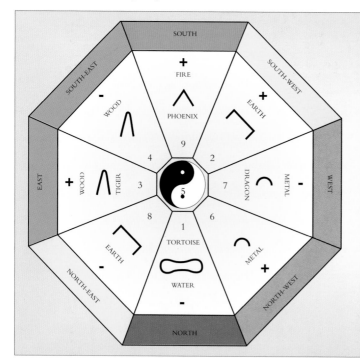

THE BAGUA, OR PA KUA

This diagram shows the energies associated with each of the eight directions. The outer bar shows the colours and directions associated with the five elements. The symbols indicate the yin (-) or yang (+) quality of the element associated with each direction. Also shown are the shapes associated with each element. The four symbolic animals which represent the energy of each of the four cardinal directions – north, south, east, west – are indicated, and the numbers of the Magic Square are shown in their associated directions. We take on the characteristics of a number and the energies associated with it, which are thought to shape who we are, where we feel comfortable, and our fortunes. The Chinese compass is always drawn facing south since this is the favoured direction for houses to face in parts of China. This does not affect the actual magnetic north-south directions.

FINDING YOUR MAGIC NUMBER

To complete the picture, it is necessary to discover how human beings fit into the scheme. Each person is allocated a "magic" number that enables them to position themselves to their best advantage. Before finding our number from the tables opposite, we must check the date of the Chinese New Year from the "Chinese Animals Table". The previous year is used if our birthday falls before the start of the new year.

▼ *Each of the magic numbers represents a particular type of energy suggested by the annual nature cycle. Find your number on the table and discover your energy below.*

ENERGY OF NUMBERS

1: Water. Winter. Independent. Intuitive
2: Earth. Late Summer. Methodical.
3: Thunder. Spring. Progressive
4: Wind. Late Spring. Adaptable.
5: Earth. Central Force. Assertive.
6: Heaven. Late Autumn. Unyielding.
7: Lake. Autumn. Flexible. Nervous.
8: Mountain. Late Winter. Obstinate. Energetic.
9. Fire. Summer. Impulsive. Intelligent.

USING THE MAGIC NUMBERS

Some Feng Shui consultants use only the male, or yang, numbers in their calculations, some use both male and female, or yin, numbers. Others regard the yin (female) numbers as depicting the inner self, while the yang (male) numbers represent the image a person presents to the world. Traditional male and female stereotypes are no longer the norm. Modern men and women, with more interchangeable roles, tend to have both yin and yang characteristics.

EAST-WEST DIRECTIONS

People tend to fare better in some directions than in others. They fall into two groups, the east group or the west group. Those who fall into the east group should live in a house facing an east group direction, those in the west group a west group direction. If this is not possible, your bed and/or your chair should face an appropriate direction.

▼ *Once you have found your magic number, you can identify which group you are in, east or west, which directions suit you. and whether your house is compatible.*

GROUP	NUMBERS	DIRECTIONS
East	1, 3, 4, 9	N, E, SE, S
West	2, 5, 6, 7, 8	SW, NW, W, NE, CENTRE

THE MAGIC NUMBERS

YEAR	M	F	YEAR	M	F	YEAR	M	F	YEAR	M	F
1920	8	7	1952	3	3	1984	7	8	2002	7	8
1921	7	8	1953	2	4	1985	6	9	2003	6	9
1922	6	9	1954	1	5	1986	5	1	2004	5	1
1923	5	1	1955	9	6	1987	4	2	2005	4	2
1924	4	2	1956	8	7	1988	3	3	2006	3	3
1925	3	3	1957	7	8	1989	2	4	2007	2	4
1926	2	4	1958	6	9	1990	1	5	2008	1	5
1927	1	5	1959	5	1	1991	9	6	2009	9	6
1928	9	6	1960	4	2	1992	8	7	2010	8	7
1929	8	7	1961	3	3	1993	7	8	2011	7	8
1930	7	8	1962	2	4	1994	6	9	2012	6	9
1931	6	9	1963	1	5	1995	5	1	2013	5	1
1932	5	1	1964	9	6	1996	4	2	2014	4	2
1933	4	2	1965	8	7	1997	3	3	2015	3	3
1934	3	3	1966	7	8	1998	2	4	2016	2	4
1935	2	4	1967	6	9	1999	1	5	2017	1	5
1936	1	5	1968	5	1	2000	9	6	2018	9	6
1937	9	6	1969	4	2	2001	8	7	2019	8	7
1938	8	7	1970	3	3						
1939	7	8	1971	2	4						
1940	6	9	1972	1	5						
1941	5	1	1973	9	6						
1942	4	2	1974	8	7						
1943	3	3	1975	7	8						
1944	2	4	1976	6	9						
1945	1	5	1977	5	1						
1946	9	6	1978	4	2						
1947	8	7	1979	3	3						
1948	7	8	1980	2	4						
1949	6	9	1981	1	5						
1950	5	1	1982	9	6						
1951	4	2	1983	8	7						

Key: M = male F = female

▼ *A Chinese Feng Shui expert studies the luo pan (compass).*

PERCEPTION AND THE SYMBOLIC BAGUA

Much of the skill in undertaking a Feng Shui survey of our immediate environment is in reading the signals there. If we are healthy and happy, this may prove to be a comparatively easy process. If we are not, our perception may be coloured by our emotional or physical state and we may not be able to see things clearly.

The Chinese phrase "First, luck; second, destiny; third, Feng Shui; fourth, virtues; fifth, education" is worth repeating, as it shows that to some extent our fortunes and personalities are out of our hands. If we embrace Feng Shui, think and act positively, and make use of the knowledge the universe has to offer, then we can begin to take charge of the parts of our lives that we can control and make the best of them.

Part of the process of Feng Shui is to awaken our senses and sensibilities to our environment. Among other things, each of the Five Elements governs different senses, and our aim is to create a balanced environment in which all our senses are satisfied and none is allowed to predominate over the rest to create an imbalance.

We can heighten our perception of the world if we introduce ourselves to different experiences. Take an objective look at your weekly routine and decide on a new experience or activity which will add something different to your life.

A MAGICAL TEMPLATE

When Feng Shui began to take off in the West several years ago, the workings of the compass were known only to a handful of scholars. Those early days were distinguished by the creation of, and endless discussions on, the workings of the Bagua. It was used then, as it is now, by the Tibetan Black Hat practitioners, as a magical template that is aligned with a front door, the entrance to a room, the front of a desk or even a face.

This template is then used to supply information which can enable us to understand our energy and make corrections to create balance and harmony. Some Chinese practitioners have since

A HEALTHY LIFESTYLE AND A HEALTHY MIND

Stuck energy in our homes is often a reflection of our lifestyle and state of mind. A healthy daily regime will make us receptive to the powers of Feng Shui.

Ideally, we should take time out each day to meditate – or just to escape from stress. Often a short walk, gardening or a few minutes sitting quietly will help us to relax. Holidays and new experiences can help our mental energy.

Chi Kung and T'ai Chi are part of the same system. Their exercise programmes help to keep the energy channels in the body unblocked, while also releasing the mind.

Eating a healthy balanced diet of food-stuffs, produced without chemical interference, is another way of ensuring that harmful energies, or toxins, do not upset our bodily balance.

If we do become ill, acupuncture and acupressure and Chinese herbal medicine can balance the energies in our bodies and help to keep us fit.

◀ *Meditation (left), hiking in the mountains (bottom left) or a daily session of T'ai Chi (bottom right) will all benefit our mental energy and help to heighten our perceptions.*

▲ *Mountains afford protection to the rear and sides of this village, while a lake in front accumulates chi – all that remains is to arrange the inside of the house to create a supportive environment.*

sought to use the Bagua alongside the compass method. They place it over the plan of a home so that it is positioned with the Career area in the north, irrespective of where the front door lies.

Other traditional Chinese approaches concentrate on interpreting the energies indicated by the Five Elements and by the rings of the luo pan. Such is the "magic" of Feng Shui that, in the right hands, all approaches appear to work.

Newcomers to Feng Shui may find it difficult to connect to a compass. Hopefully, they will use either method to experience for themselves the magic of the early days of discovery, and will be drawn deeper into this amazing philosophy, gaining an insight into its power.

▼ *The Three Gates Bagua. This may be entered through "Career" (back), "Knowledge" (bottom left) or "Helpful People" (bottom right). The compass Bagua with associated colours is shown inside to help you balance the elements of your home.*

THE SYMBOLIC BAGUA

Throughout this book we will see how various images are connected to each of the eight points of the Magic Square or the Bagua, which is based on it. The symbolic Bagua uses the energies of each direction to relate to the journey of life. The journey begins at the entrance to our home – the mouth of chi – and moves in a predetermined way through the home until it reaches its conclusion. By focusing on an aspect of our lives which we want to stimulate or change, we can use the energies of the universe and make them work for us. Psychologically, focusing on an area enables us to create the circumstances to bring about change.

So far, a traditional compass approach has been used, but the diagram to the left allows us to use either approach. From now on readers should feel free to connect with the Bagua as they wish, and through it to the intangible forces which make this such a fascinating subject. Most people who have used Feng Shui have experienced changes in their circumstances. These often correspond to the actual energy around a relationship or situation rather than our desires. The results will ultimately serve our best interests, but the outcome is often unexpected.

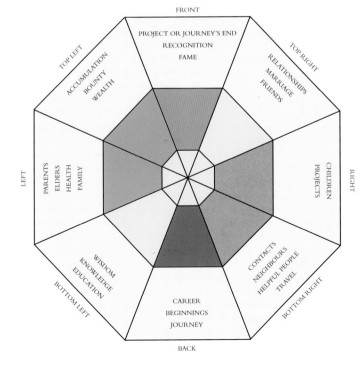

FRONT

PROJECT OR JOURNEY'S END
RECOGNITION
FAME

TOP LEFT

ACCUMULATION
BOUNTY
WEALTH

TOP RIGHT

RELATIONSHIPS
MARRIAGE
FRIENDS

LEFT

PARENTS
ELDERS
HEALTH
FAMILY

RIGHT

CHILDREN
PROJECTS

WISDOM
KNOWLEDGE
EDUCATION

BOTTOM LEFT

CAREER
BEGINNINGS
JOURNEY

CONTACTS
NEIGHBOURS
HELPFUL PEOPLE
TRAVEL

BOTTOM RIGHT

BACK

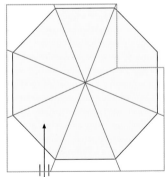

▲ *The Three Gates Bagua is flexible. If a home has an irregular shape, the corresponding area of the Bagua is also considered to be missing. In this house, the front entrance is in the "Knowledge" area and the "Relationships" part of the house is missing.*

FENG SHUI IN THE MODERN WORLD

Modern lifestyles are far removed from those of our ancestors. For them, charting the progress of the moon and sun, and interpreting the different weather conditions and other activities occurring in the natural world in relation to the movement of the stars and planets,

▲ *Night-time in Mexico City. The 23 million inhabitants are denied a view of the stars because of neon lighting and pollution.*

▶ *The rice harvest in traditional regions of China has used many of the same processes for the past thousand years.*

▼ *There are still thriving cultures in which ancient skills and lifestyles remain such as this village in Chad.*

was essential. These peoples depended on the land to provide them with the means to survive. The modern city-dweller may never see food growing naturally and may not even be able to view the night sky because of pollution and neon lighting. However, we still depend on the natural world for our well-being. We can be at the mercy of hurricanes, or bask on sun-drenched beaches; mountains may erupt, or provide sustenance for livestock; human beings can pollute the air and contaminate the land, or create sanctuaries for wildlife species.

Ancient peoples, through necessity, regarded the heavens, the earth and themselves as part of one system. This holistic view of life has persisted in many cultures, where health and medicine, food and lifestyle are all interconnected. In the West, scientific development created different disciplines which advanced in isolation from each other. Through recent movements in health and food production, we are seeking to correct the imbalances caused by this approach. The Tao, or the Way, the philosophy which underlies Feng Shui, shows how it is possible to order our lives to exist in harmony with each other and the natural world. We can use Feng Shui to help us work towards achieving this.

The traditional concept of Gaia, the Greek earth goddess, was used by James Lovelock and Lynne Margulis in the 1970s to encourage us to perceive the world as a biosphere in which each constituent part has a role to play. In order to understand Feng Shui we need to expand this concept of ecosystems further to include human beings and the impact of

▲ *In 1948 science writer Fred Hoyle predicted: "Once a photograph of the Earth taken from the outside world is available ... a new idea as powerful as any other in history will be let loose." The environmental awareness movement began at the time human beings landed on the moon.*

WORKING WITH THE NATURAL WORLD

A good example of working with the natural world is provided by an apparently admirable scheme to plant 300 oak forests in Britain to celebrate the millennium. But in the natural world oak trees grow singly and not in rows in large groups, and recent research has indicated that where many oaks grow together there is a higher incidence of Lyme disease, a debilitating illness which attacks the nervous system. The reason for this is that mice and deer feed on acorns and also carry the ticks which transmit the disease. Thus, where there are many oaks, there is also a high incidence of Lyme disease. Mixed planting, which mirrors the natural world, would be preferable.

In order to save money, one forest was planted with Polish oak trees that came into bud two weeks later than the native trees. This meant there were no caterpillars feeding on the buds to provide food for newly-hatched fledglings. These mistakes might have been avoided if Taoistic principles had been applied to the scheme.

▼ *Native trees act as the Tortoise, Dragon, Tiger formation to protect these buildings.*

the cosmos, and to expand our awareness so that we can predict the consequences of our actions.

As we investigate the ideas behind Feng Shui and consider practical ways of introducing them into our lives, we also need to shift our perception. Feng Shui in the modern world incorporates intuition. Maori warriors navigate hundreds of miles by the feel of a place and by observing signs. The Inuit language incorporates many words to describe the complexities of different types of snow. Similarly, we can heighten our awareness of our environment by adopting the principles of Feng Shui.

Until recently navigators used the stars to steer by, and in some parts of the world those who work with the land still use the stars to determine planting times for their crops. These people recognize patterns in the interrelationship between different parts of the natural world, noticing which plants are in flower or when birds return from migration and comparing them to the weather. Many customs are firmly based in natural wisdom.

FENG SHUI
IN THE
HOME

WHEREVER WE LIVE, IN THE TOWN OR THE
COUNTRY, WE CAN ARRANGE OUR IMMEDIATE
ENVIRONMENT SO THAT WE RECEIVE MAXIMUM
SUPPORT. SOME HOUSES INSTINCTIVELY "FEEL"
RIGHT AND A LUO PAN READING WILL USUALLY
CONFIRM THIS. OTHER HOMES MAY NOT, AND
SOMETIMES EXTERNAL INFLUENCES CAN
ADVERSELY AFFECT BENEFICIAL ENERGY.
THE FOLLOWING PAGES OFFER SOLUTIONS TO
HELP YOU TO BE NOURISHED BY YOUR HOME.

THE
OUTSIDE
WORLD

—

We need to feel comfortable inside our homes but
sometimes the external environment impinges upon us.
Perhaps the view from the windows is unattractive or the
traffic is noisy. We are aware of such things but there may
also be other influences that affect us psychologically over
a period of time. Our physical health can also be harmed
by more subtle forces that we cannot see. Feng Shui can
identify these influences and forces for us, and can help us
to take precautionary measures. When we move house,
we can use the information we have gained to
show us what to look for.

CHOOSING A LOCATION

Whether we own our own home or apartment or live in rented accommodation, we can use the principles which follow to create a living space in which we feel comfortable. If we are on the verge of moving, or are in the fortunate position of having acquired a piece of land to design and build our own home upon, there are some important considerations to make. You will probably already have a location in mind, but within the area there will be choices you can make which will affect your well-being in your new home.

When choosing a property we normally investigate the immediate environment. We use certain criteria to judge it according to our individual requirements – the appearance of neighbouring properties, proximity to schools, efficient transport for travel to work, green spaces, sports facilities and so on.

Some moves are dictated by new jobs in different areas, some when people give up their hectic urban lifestyles and relocate to rural areas. Many older people retire to the coast. Young people leaving home for the first time might be

▲ *The modern city of Durban in South Africa is full of young energy.*

▶ *A seaside location is very attractive in summer but can be inhospitable in winter.*

▼ *Living on a remote farm will suit some people perfectly, but not others.*

attracted by the hurly-burly of city living. The decline of heavy industry in many countries has seen a rise in the regeneration of dockland and riverside areas with large warehouses being developed as spacious apartments for these new city dwellers. Whatever the reason for the move, few people remain where they were born, or retain the extended support networks which prevailed only a generation or two ago. Our choice of home as a nurturing space is therefore important. With a little foresight and a knowledge of Feng Shui principles, we can select prime positions for our homes.

THINK BEFORE YOU MOVE

There are certain things to consider when selecting an area to which to move before we even consider choosing a house. Ideally we should know the area well. An idyllic bay in summer may be cold and windswept in winter, and a woodland glade at the end of an unmade track may be inaccessible after heavy winter snows.

Neighbours can prove to be a problem. They may resent a new house which spoils a view, or may erect screens that maintain their privacy but deprive you of

ASSESSING A LOCATION

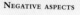

NATURAL PHENOMENA	IMMEDIATE ENVIRONMENT	POSITIVE ASPECTS	NEGATIVE ASPECTS
Wind direction	Proposed road developments	Local amenities	Factories
Sun direction	Proposed building developments	Trees	Petrol stations
Rainfall	Land use plans	Street lighting	All-night cafés
Flood areas	Previous land use	Good street maintenance	Pubs and discos
Geological faults	Tree preservation orders	Good schools	Police stations
Soil type	Local architecture	Community spirit	Fire stations
Height above sea level	Neighbours, predecessors	Local shops	Airports
		Clubs and classes	Cemeteries and crematoriums
		Playgroups and nurseries	Motorways and highways
			Electricity sub-stations and pylons

◀ *This sheltered village is a delightful location to return home to after a day in the bustling city.*

▶ *High-rise flats in Hong Kong – financially the sky is the limit and young people are attracted there, but few of them stay to put down roots.*

light. It is important to determine the ownership of boundaries. Previous owners are another consideration. Earlier occupants may have tipped chemicals just where you want to grow strawberries, or you may learn that all the previous owners got divorced or mysteriously contracted a similar illness. Feng Shui may be able to offer an explanation. The box above indicates some things to check before moving to a new area.

The modern world has problems that

▼ *Pavement cafés are part of metropolitan life in many cities around the world.*

did not exist in the ancient world and these must be taken into consideration when we apply Feng Shui today. It is no use selecting a site with the classic Tortoise, Dragon, Tiger formation if the Tortoise is an electricity pylon, which may be linked to childhood leukemia, the Dragon is a chemical factory leaking its waste into the river, and the Tiger is a poorly managed petrol station. In modern times we have to apply the formulae to contemporary life and the ancient sages were wise enough to allow us the leeway to do this by building in formulae for change.

Our environment makes a psychological impact on us: whatever we see, hear or smell will make an impression. We also have to look at ourselves and what type of people we are in order to understand our needs in terms of living spaces. There is no point moving to a remote country area if you enjoy street life and love shopping because you will never feel comfortable. A Rabbit who retires to the

seaside will, at best, be tired and drained and, at worst, become ill. With a new insight into our own natures and increased awareness of the effect our environment has on us, we can use Feng Shui principles to find harmonious spaces for ourselves and our families.

When you are ready to sell your home and move on, Feng Shui can help to speed up this often lengthy and stressful process. The tip below combines the energy of the Five Elements to give a powerful boost to the sale.

FENG SHUI TIP FOR SPEEDING UP A HOUSE SALE

Take a red envelope and place in it:

◆ A piece of metal from the kitchen
◆ Some earth from the garden
◆ Some wood from a skirting board

Throw the envelope into a fast-moving river.

UNSEEN ENERGIES

Before finally deciding on a location, it is wise to check if there are any underground water sources, geological faults or other earth disturbances. These all create unseen energies which could affect your well-being.

GEOPATHIC STRESS

The word "geopathic" comes from the Greek *geo*, meaning "Earth", and *pathos*, meaning "disease". It covers naturally occurring phenomena that cause problems for us and our homes. The Earth and living organisms vibrate at complementary frequencies, which are negatively affected by geopathic faults. Dowsers are able to detect these problems, which a property surveyor may miss.

UNDERGROUND STREAMS

Just as water erodes rocks on the coast, underground streams have had the same effect beneath the Earth's surface. This process alters the electromagnetic frequency of the Earth so that it is out of our frequency range. Fast-moving and polluted underground water produces the same effect.

Underground streams produce energy spirals, the effects of which are felt inside

▲ *If trees lean for no reason, they may be situated on a geopathic stress line.*

any buildings directly overhead. Where a clockwise spiral meets an anti-clockwise spiral, ill health may be experienced by people situated above them. Where spirals meet other forces, such as leys, the problems are accentuated.

LEYS

Leys, or ley lines, are a network of surface energy lines running across the countryside. Our distant ancestors may have built their churches and standing stones on these lines, performing an "acupuncture of the Earth" as they tapped into its energy. It is believed the leys also provided routes for travellers.

▲ *Underground water creates magical places, but it is not desirable near a house as it can undermine the foundations.*

◄ *Stone circles are extremely powerful places. They harness the Earth's energies and respond to those of the Cosmos.*

▲ *The Chinese believe that quarrying damages the Dragon – the spirit of a place.*

▲ *Nearby railway lines can cause land disturbance and create instability.*

earth is covered by a series of force lines which are activated by the interaction of the Earth's magnetic field and the gravitational pull of the sun and moon. It is thought that these lines shift as a result of their interaction with the movement of charged particles trapped in the atmosphere as the sun blasts the Earth with radiation. The point where these lines cross may adversely affect the human body.

HUMAN ACTIVITY

Human beings can also disturb the Earth's energies. Quarries, tunnels, mines, polluted water and railways have all been found to contribute negative effects. Before erecting or buying a house, check for any mining or tunnelling that may have taken place in the area.

RADON

We are exposed to radiation throughout our lives, mainly from the sun. Exposure over long periods to higher than normal levels may make us ill. Leukemia and birth defects have been linked to exposure to radon, which occurs naturally in uranium in the Earth. As the uranium breaks down, it forms radioactive ions which attach themselves to air particles that become trapped inside houses. Some regions in the world have recorded

levels of radioactivity in excess of those recorded after the Chernobyl disaster. Pockets of high incidence have been found in Sweden and the United States as well as in Derbyshire and Cornwall in Great Britain. Local authorities are aware of the problem and assistance is available to eradicate it from buildings.

EARTH GRIDS

Two German doctors, Hartmann and Curry, have advanced the theory that the

---

STRESS INDICATORS
Leaning trees
Cankers on tree trunks
Elder trees
Illness shortly after moving
Uneasy atmosphere
Tunnelling activity
Cold, damp rooms

CLEARING THE ENERGIES

If there is no apparent reason for feeling unwell for a long period of time, then geopathic stress is a possible cause. Experienced dowsers are able to detect Earth energies and, in some instances, divert negative energies, albeit often only on a temporary basis. Many people can detect water with rods or pendulums, but experience is needed to deal with Earth energies and protection is needed to minimize ill effects. It is best, if possible, to move away from such energies, and it may be a question of simply moving a bed 60 cm–1 m (2–3 ft). The effect of clearing energies can be dramatic and can even cause shock. When dealing with heart patients, for example, the work should be done slowly.

▲ *Dowsing rods are part of a Feng Shui consultant's tools. Metal coat hangers also work for dowsing.*

▲ *Dowsing rods cross when they detect underground water. They are used to locate landmines and to find pipes.*

THE URBAN ENVIRONMENT

Urban environments are very diverse. Living in an apartment above a shop in a city centre throbbing with nightlife is quite different to the tranquillity of a house in a leafy suburb or the vast buildings in a redeveloped docklands area.

CITY AND TOWN CENTRES
The centres of large cities, where clubs and restaurants are open through the night, are full of yang energy and lifestyles will reflect this. City centres attract younger people with no roots, who can move about freely. Homes tend to be apartments and inside we should aim for some yin energy – muted colours, natural flooring and a large plant or two to create a quiet haven. Smaller town centres, particularly where there are shopping precincts, tend to close down at night and the atmosphere is yin and rather spooky. If you live here, make sure you have plenty of lights on the perimeter of your property and bright colours inside to prevent feeling closed in.

PARKS AND SPACES
These green oases are somehow apart from the bustling city centre. Homes are usually expensive and sought after, since

▲ *An enticing night scene in Villefranche, Cote d'Azur, France. Summer in the city can be envigorating and exciting.*

they provide tranquil spaces and fresh air while still connected to the life of the city. People residing here will have more stable lifestyles as they have the yin-yang

▼ *Suburban living at its best in Sag Harbour, New York; wide streets, mature trees and no parked cars.*

balance. Their homes should reflect this with a mixture of stimulating shapes, colours and materials, plus restful spaces.

DOCKLANDS
The energy of docklands is interesting. The yang energy of the large converted warehouses contrasts with the daytime yin energy when the occupants, usually young executives, are at work. At weekends this changes as café life and boating activities take over. Docklands are usually on main traffic routes, so on weekdays there is often stuck energy. Large trees should be planted to help cope with the pollution, and also to bring yin energy into the area. Rooms tend to be huge and it is difficult to ground the energy. Cosy yin spaces need to be created within the vast expanse to offer support. Large plants will also help the yin-yang balance.

SUBURBS
The energy in the suburbs is mainly yin, with little nightlife. People tend to hide and become insular in suburbs, and often a yang balance is required. Imaginative use of colour is often all that is required to raise the energy of suburban homes.

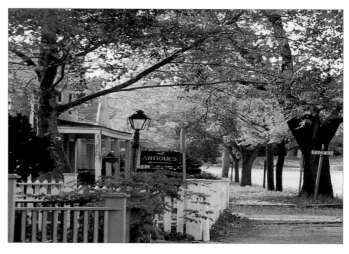

ROADS

Roads conduct chi through an environment and transport patterns can affect the nature of a neighbourhood. Living close to urban highways is an obvious health risk, but so too is living on narrow suburban "rat runs". Chi travels fast on straight urban roads and thus residents will not relax easily. In the United States, where suburban roads are built on a grid system, large gardens compensate and help to maintain a balance. Check the transport patterns before purchasing a new home and visit at different times of the day. Well-designed cul-de-sacs have excellent chi, but those where car movement has not been well planned create stuck energy and danger for children playing there.

The visual impact of a flyover in a residential area can be devastating. The fast-moving traffic conducts chi away from the area and will greatly affect the fortunes of those living at eye level or underneath the flyover.

RAILWAYS

The effect of a railway is similar to a motorway in that trains carry chi away from an area, particularly if they are at the end of the garden. Trains also create slight unease in the expectation of their arrival. Underground trains are destabilizing if they pass immediately below houses. If systems are old and poorly maintained the Chinese saying "Angry Dragons waiting to erupt" applies.

▼ *Parks and green areas are an important part of city life. This park is located in Adelaide, Australia.*

ROADS AND CHI

Today roads serve as conductors of chi. Steadily moving traffic on curving roads near our homes is beneficial. Fast traffic and roads pointing at us are not.

THE CURVING ROAD The road gently curves and appears to "hug" this house. This is a very auspicious Feng Shui position for a dwelling.

THE BENDING ROAD House B is in an inauspicious position. Traffic from both directions may break suddenly at the bend and could hit the house. At night, car beams will illuminate the rooms. There will always be a negative air of expectancy here. Convex mirrors on the outer bend would be the usual solution, but they would deflect and deplete the energy of the auspicious house A. Instead, a better solution would be to have traffic-calming measures in place as shown.

THE FAST ROAD This creates a visual and psychological barrier. Waist-high shrubs and plants on the boundary of the garden and plants on the windowsill inside the houses will slow down the chi. Those living at the junction of such roads are likely to be jumpy. Screeching brakes and even crashes are common at such points.

THE DEAD-END ROAD The house facing the entrance is at risk since the chi seems to hurtle towards it, as at a T-junction. Deflection is needed, and a hedge would help. An alternative would be to build a porch with the door at the side. Mirrors are often used to return the harmful influence back on itself. If the path to the door faces the road, it would be better to move and curve it. The effect is the same where a bridge points at a house. Residents will feel exhausted in such a location.

THE KNIFE The road appears to cut into the apartments like a knife. The constant flow past the window will leave residents tetchy. A mirror outside will symbolically deflect the problem. Coloured glass in the windows facing the road would block the unattractive view whilst allowing light in.

THE FLYOVER Residents here will feel overwhelmed and apprehensive. Lights on the corners of the house will symbolically lift the flyover, but this is not a good house to live in. Residents will feel oppressed and have no energy.

RURAL LOCATIONS

The energies found in the country-side are quite different to those of urban areas, but just as powerful. By carefully positioning our homes within the natural features of the landscape we can draw on their protection to nourish us.

COUNTRY LIVING

A sheltered position contained by trees or hills is ideal, especially in remote areas where protection from the elements is very important in winter. The classical arrangement of the four animals is the perfect site but if there are no woods or mountains where you wish to live, large trees and buildings can also act as protectors. Road access is vital in rural areas but, as in towns, it is preferable not to live close to major roads or through routes.

BENEFICIAL LOCATIONS

A tree belt behind acts as the Tortoise, and hedges represent the Dragon and Tiger. The Dragon is higher to keep the unpredictable Tiger in its place. A small hill in the foreground acts as the Phoenix.

A stream feeding a healthy pond is auspicious. Shrubs hide the water's exit from the property.

▲ *This lovely Mediterranean-style house is positioned in a supportive rural setting.*

Even if you live out in the wild, it is important to have a social centre within reach. Out-of-town superstores have knocked the heart out of many country towns and villages, and have made an impact on the chi of these places, but those that continue to thrive usually have an excellent yin-yang balance. They provide sport and leisure facilities for young people and a good community life, which are the yang activities in the yin setting of the countryside.

In the fields and woods, chi is good and there are many opportunities to restore the balance in our busy modern lives. Intensive farming methods can be harmful, however, so look out for telltale signs such as few songbirds or no hedges before purchasing a property.

POSITIVE ASPECTS	POSSIBLE NEGATIVE ASPECTS
Natural smells	Agrochemicals
Leisurely pace of life	Isolation
Walks	Flooding
Trees	Travel distances & access
Wildlife	Limited public transport
Fresh food	Landfill
Air quality	Military training areas
Relaxed lifestyle	Bad weather
Outdoor life	Effluent pipes
Happy people	Amenities closed in winter

RIVERS AND LAKES

Energy is usually very good near water, especially near slow-flowing rivers that meander through the countryside. Proportion is important, so if the water is balanced by an undulating landscape and plenty of green vegetation it will feel comfortable. A stream feeding into a healthy pond is ideal as it will accumulate chi and also attract wildlife to visit your garden. The energy near lakes is different, reflecting the breathless movement of the wind across the water and the sudden appearance and disappearance of water sports activities at weekends.

If you decide to live in a flood plain you will need to make enquiries about the likelihood of floods in the area, especially following those of recent years.

COASTAL AREAS

Being beside the sea gives most of us a sense of well-being. This is partly due to the beneficial effects of negative ions in the air, which create an invigorating atmosphere. Waves can, however, adversely affect some people, depending on their animal sign – Rabbits, for example, tend to feel uneasy near the sea.

▲ *A house situated next to a slow-moving river will benefit from good chi flow.*

In the summer, the teeming beaches full of holiday-makers are yang. In winter the towering seas are also yang, but the deserted seaside towns and isolated bays are yin. It is a good idea to visit the area in both seasons as they are so different. The elements of wind and water are never so much in evidence as when the storms lash the sea against the rocks. A peninsula is difficult to live on because the chi there dissipates in the winter when it is hammered by the elements.

▶ *A tranquil bay in summer looks very different in winter.*

ROADS TO HOME

Living in rural areas may mean that you have to commute to work and spend quite some time in the car. The daily journey you make, and the roads on which you travel, will have a considerable impact on your life, so check both when considering your new home.

Where trees overhang a road they can afford a welcome relief from the glaring sun. However, long stretches may cause nausea and headaches brought on by the flickering, dappled light.

Travelling to work in an easterly direction in the morning and returning in a westerly direction with the sun glaring on the windscreen could affect our moods considerably. This can be particularly dangerous on narrow roads.

Wonderful views can make us feel euphoric and energized, although care must be taken not to lose concentration when driving. Scenic roads can be tricky in adverse weather conditions.

Narrow country lanes with high banks or hedges funnel chi and afford no relief for the driver. Where they twist and turn, the driver's vision is extremely limited. Regular use will become a strain.

HOUSE STYLES

The position of our homes within their environment and how they fit in with the surrounding buildings can affect how comfortable we are living there. At a simple level, if our home is a big detached house in a road of smaller terraced houses, then we will be set apart from the rest of the community. Similarly, if the house is very different in style from its neighbours it will not fit into its environment. Strict planning laws in some

▼ *This painted house is not in sympathy with its neighbours.*

▲ *A balance of Metal, suggested by the circular lawn, and Water in the curved path.*

areas have preserved the "spirit" or chi of towns and villages, and such places tend to have a sense of community. On the other hand, where building has been unrestricted and tall blocks spring up between two-storey houses with no regard for the character of the environment, then the area's chi dissipates and its sense of community is lost.

When we make alterations to our houses or decorate them, we should be mindful of the impact on the neighbourhood. If ours is the only stucco house in a row of brick houses, we isolate ourselves and change the chi of the area. If all the houses in the neighbourhood are of a certain era and we decide

BALANCING THE ELEMENTS

ELEMENT	HELPED BY	HARMED BY	WEAKENED BY	WEAKENS
Wood	Water	Metal	Fire	Earth
Fire	Wood	Water	Earth	Metal
Earth	Fire	Wood	Metal	Water
Metal	Earth	Fire	Water	Wood
Water	Metal	Earth	Wood	Fire

▲ *The intrusive tower blocks have completely changed the nature of this area.*

to change the style of the windows or substantially alter the architectural detail, we again damage the energy of the environment. Doors, chimney stacks and porches all add to the character and overall proportion not only of our house, but of the neighbourhood.

HOUSE SHAPES

The best-shaped house is square. It is well proportioned and is the symbolic shape for Earth, which gathers, supports and nourishes. Rectangular buildings are also well regarded. An L-shaped building is considered inauspicious since it is said to resemble a meat cleaver and the worst position to have a room is in the "blade". If a teenager has a room in this position, they may feel isolated and may get up to all sorts of things undetected. An older

WOOD: Tall thin apartment blocks and offices are often Wood-shaped.

FIRE: Fire buildings have pyramid-shaped or pointed roofs.

METAL: Metal buildings have domed roofs; the shape of these African homes is mirrored in Western churches.

EARTH: Earth-shaped buildings are long and low such as bungalows.

FIRE: Wood-shaped windows and Earth-shaped lines give balance.

WATER: Water buildings are those which have had sections added to them over the years in a random pattern.

BUILDINGS AND THE FIVE ELEMENTS

FIVE ELEMENT CURES FOR CORRECTING IMBALANCES

WOOD: Posts, pillars, tower-shaped plant supports, green walls, trees
FIRE: Pyramid-shaped finials, wigwam-shaped plant supports, garden buildings with Fire-shaped roofs, red walls, lights
EARTH: Straight hedges, rectangular garden buildings, flat-topped trellis, terracotta troughs, or terracotta walls
METAL: Round finials, round weather vanes, metal balls, white walls
WATER: Wavy hedges, water features, black or blue walls

relative with such a room may feel unwanted. Where houses are not a uniform shape, we need to make them more regular, as we will investigate later.

ORIENTATION
The direction in which a building faces will also affect its chi. North-facing buildings with the main windows at the front will feel cheerless since they will not

receive any sun. The energy can become stagnant and it is important to warm the house with colour. Houses with the main windows facing south and south-west will receive strong yang energy and will need cool colours to compensate. Houses facing east receive early morning sun and vibrant energy. In the west, the energy is falling. Directions determine room placement within the house.

ENTRANCES, PATHS AND FRONT DOORS

The entrance to our home is very important. It represents the image we present to the world and can indicate the view we have of ourselves. When we return to our home, we need to be drawn into our own nurturing space through a pleasant environment, however small. If we live in an apartment, we need to distinguish our own special part of the block and make it unique, by using a colourful doormat, introducing plants or by other means.

ENTRANCES

Front gardens can fill up with an accumulation of stagnant energy unless we are careful. In house conversions where the grounds are not managed, the situation can be difficult since no-one is in overall charge of the garden. As a result, packaging, old furniture, chunks of wood and other assorted rubbish can pile up. Often, dustbins are sited in the front garden and can seriously affect how we feel when we return home. Bins should be placed away

▲ *Tree guardians mark the entrance to this attractive house. The effect that is created is very welcoming.*

from the front entrance, preferably behind a hedge or fencing. If one resident clears up, others may follow suit.

PATHS

These should gently meander through the garden to enable us to unwind at the end of a long day, or to welcome us back from a trip. Straight paths from the street to the front door carry chi too quickly and we do not have time to change gear. Ideally there should be an open space in front of the entrance where the chi can gather, but often these are filled with parked cars and there is no distinction

▼ *A meandering path enables us to shed the cares of the day before arriving home.*

ENTRANCES

◄ This tree is overpowering the house. A convex mirror on the front door or a polished door knob will disperse its energy. Gateposts symbolically reverse the flow and send it back to the tree.

▼ This tree blocks the gap between the two opposite houses. Such gaps symbolically represent money escaping.

▼ This house illustrates a situation known as "long eye", which can cause health problems.

▼ Counteract "long eye" by ensuring both eyes have the same focal length. Placing trees as shown is one way.

PATHS

▲ Straight paths to the front door funnel chi too quickly to and from the house.

▲ Ideally, garden paths should meander to the front door to slow down the energy.

▲ Narrowing paths of this shape funnel chi too quickly into our homes.

▲ Paths this shape resemble a jug pouring away from the house and disperse chi.

between home and work. Squeezing past a car to enter the house is claustrophobic, as are very small enclosed porches, creating restriction which may be mirrored in our approach to life.

FRONT DOORS

These should be well-maintained and clean. A tub of plants on either side is welcoming but they should not restrict the space. House numbers should be visible by day and night and doorbells should be in working order to maintain

◄ *Plants either side of the poles would improve these well-maintained apartments.*

harmonious relationships with callers. The chi of an area can be severely depleted if visitors whistle, shout or use their car horns. Door colours should reflect the compass direction they face and be balanced according to the Five Elements.

DEPARTING

What we see when we leave our homes can also colour our day. Large objects like telegraph poles and trees directly in line with the front door send "poison arrows" of chi at the house, as do the corners of other buildings. If tall hedges or fences restrict our vision from the house we may become insular or feel depressed.

▼ *A balance of the Five Elements, but taller plants would improve the proportion.*

▼ *A plant pot on the left would help to balance this front entrance.*

▼ *The Metal-shaped pot plants on either side of this door are full of energy.*

INSIDE
THE HOME

—

Once you have found a suitable location, make sure that your house is facing a supportive direction and then turn your attention to the interior. Even if the external environment is less than perfect, you can still maximize the potential of your home by choosing suitable rooms for different activities and decorating them appropriately. Using Feng Shui, you can enhance specific areas of your home and thus improve certain aspects of your life that you are not satisfied with.

BENEFICIAL POSITIONS

Having selected a protected site in which to live, it is desirable that the house is orientated in what is considered in Feng Shui to be an auspicious direction which will support its occupants. Those who fall into the east category should face their houses toward the east directions; west group people should face the west directions. It is very likely that there will be a mixture of east and west group people within a family or others sharing a house. The people who are compatible with the house will feel most comfortable in it. Others should ensure that principle rooms fall into their favoured directions or at least that beds, desks and chairs are positioned correctly.

POSITIONING YOURSELF

Once you know your "magic" numbers, it is possible to design the interior of your house so that you position yourself in directions which are beneficial to you. Beds should be orientated so that the top of your head when lying down faces one of the four beneficial locations. In the same way chairs that you sit in should also face one of your beneficial locations.

▶ *We need to relax at the end of the day. A room with windows facing west is good, or a position favoured by our "magic" number.*

▼ *We aim to locate our rooms in good directions and decorate to suit the elements.*

▲ *The compass direction your house faces is dependent on where the main entrance is, and is the starting point for positioning yourself inside the house.*

FIND YOUR BEST AND WORST DIRECTIONS

1. Check your magic number on "The Magic Numbers" table.
2. Check the "Best and Worst Directions" table to determine prime places for you to sit, sleep and work.

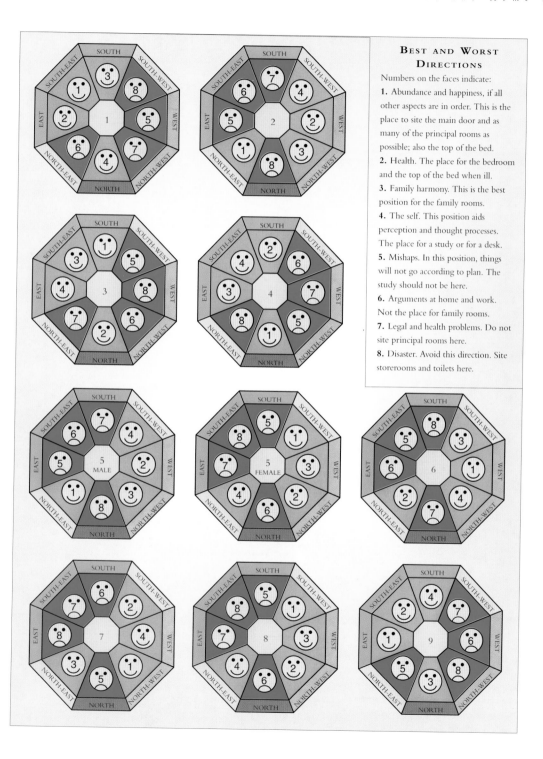

BEST AND WORST DIRECTIONS

Numbers on the faces indicate:

1. Abundance and happiness, if all other aspects are in order. This is the place to site the main door and as many of the principal rooms as possible; also the top of the bed.

2. Health. The place for the bedroom and the top of the bed when ill.

3. Family harmony. This is the best position for the family rooms.

4. The self. This position aids perception and thought processes. The place for a study or for a desk.

5. Mishaps. In this position, things will not go according to plan. The study should not be here.

6. Arguments at home and work. Not the place for family rooms.

7. Legal and health problems. Do not site principal rooms here.

8. Disaster. Avoid this direction. Site storerooms and toilets here.

DRAWING THE PLAN

I t is now possible to begin to apply the principles we have learned. In order to position ourselves to our best advantage, we need to determine the compass readings for our homes.

You Will Need

◆ A compass with the eight directions clearly marked

◆ A protractor – a circular one is best

◆ A scale plan of your home. If you own your home you will already have one. If not, it will be necessary to draw one, in which case you will also need a tape measure and graph paper

◆ A ruler

◆ A lead pencil and five coloured pencils – green, red, yellow, grey, dark blue

◆ A tracing of the Bagua with the suggested information marked on

To Draw a Plan

Using graph paper, take measurements for each floor, marking external walls, internal walls, alcoves, staircases, doors, windows and permanent fixtures such as baths, toilets, kitchen units and equipment, and fireplaces.

Take a Compass Reading

1. Remove watches, jewellery and metal objects and stand clear of cars and metal fixtures.

2. Stand with your back parallel to the front door and note the exact compass reading in degrees.

3. Note the direction, eg 125° SE, on to your plan as shown in the diagram. You are now ready to transfer the compass readings on to your Bagua drawing.

▶ *Use this table to double check that your heading in degrees corresponds with the direction your front door faces, since it is possible to misread the protractor.*

DIRECTIONS AND DEGREES	
North	337.5–22.5°
North-east	22.5–67.5°
East	67.5–112.5°
South-east	112.5–157.5°
South	157.5–202.5°
South-west	202.5–247.5°
West	247.5–292.5°
North-west	292.5–337.5°

▼ *Draw a scale plan of your home and mark on it the positions of windows, doors, alcoves and all internal fixtures and fittings as well as bed and desk positions. A compass, protractor, ruler, coloured pencils and a tracing of the Bagua diagram will allow you to survey your home.*

▼ 125° SE

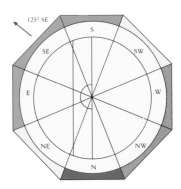

TRANSFER THE COMPASS READING TO THE BAGUA

1. Place the protractor on the Bagua diagram so that 0° is at the bottom at the north position and mark the eight directions.

2. Having found the compass reading for your home, ie the direction faced by your front door, check it matches the direction; if not you may be reading the wrong ring. Mark the position of your front door.

3. Double-check the direction by looking at the "Directions and Degrees" table. When you have done this you will end up with a Bagua diagram such as the one above, with the front door position marked. You are now almost ready to place this template on to your home plan.

EAST WEST DIRECTIONS

Just as people fit into east or west categories, so too do houses. Determine whether your house belongs to the east or west group of directions by checking the direction in which the front door faces.

EASTERN DIRECTIONS: north-east, south-east, south
WESTERN DIRECTIONS: south-west, north-west, west, north-east

East group people should preferably live in east group houses and west group people in west group houses.

TRANSFER THE DIRECTIONS TO THE PLAN

1. Find the centre of the plan. Match the main walls across the length of the plan and crease the paper lengthways.

2. Match the main walls across the width and crease the paper widthways. Where the folds cross is the centre of your home. If your home is not a perfect square or rectangle, treat a protrusion of less than 50% of the width as an extension to the direction. If the protrusion is more than 50% of the width, treat the remainder as a missing part of the direction.

3. Place the centre of the Bagua on the centre point of the plan and line up the front door position.

4. Mark the eight directions on the plan and draw in the sectors.

5. Transfer the colour markings.

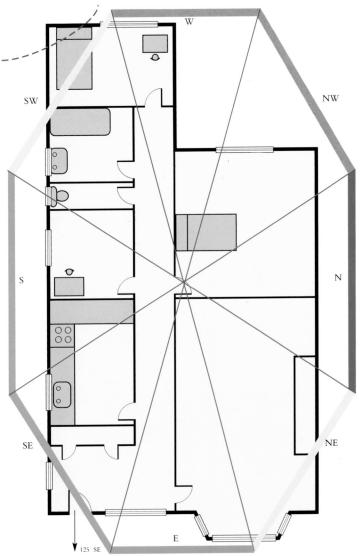

EDGES, CORNERS AND SLANTING WALLS

Certain structural details are problematic in Feng Shui. Often the result of conversions, they affect chi and can cause discomfort for the occupants of the house.

EDGES

Wherever the chi flow in a room is disrupted, difficulties occur. Anyone who has ever walked down a windy street flanked by high buildings will know that the gusts are always worse at the corners of buildings where the wind whips up into a spiral. Where major structural work has been undertaken and walls have been knocked down, a room is often left with supporting pillars. These are not conducive to the free flow of chi because they are usually square and have four corners which point, knife-like, into the room, and they can also interfere with vision.

If there are edges we should aim to soften them. Plants are one solution and fabrics are another. Wherever possible, make columns rounded as this creates an entirely different feel.

Having the edges of furniture pointing at us can make us feel uncomfortable, as can the edges of shelves and fireplaces. Keeping books in cupboards is a solution, but the pleasure of plucking a book from a shelf would be lost and the cupboards would become harbingers of tired energy. Instead, we can use plants to soften shelf edges near where we sit.

▲ *Round pillars are less obtrusive than square ones. The plant softens the effect.*

▲ *A plant will enliven an awkward corner and move the chi on.*

◀ *Plants can be used to soften shelf edges near to where we sit.*

CORNERS

The corners of rooms are often dark, so it is a good idea to place something colourful there, like a vase of silk flowers for example. Alternatively, you can use something that moves such as a lava lamp or a water feature. Putting plants in dark corners where stagnant chi accumulates will help the chi to move on. Spiky plants are particularly good provided they are away from chairs where they could direct "poison arrows" towards the occupants. Uplighters or round tables with lamps on them are other options for dark corners.

Alcoves on either side of a fireplace are often filled with shelves, which help to prevent stagnant areas provided they are not crammed full and some gaps are left.

▲ *Here, in one place, we have several methods of introducing movement into a dark corner – an octagonal table, a plant, a corner cupboard and a little shelf.*

▼ *This slanting wall will not adversely affect anyone sleeping in this room as there is plenty of headroom.*

THE FLOW OF CHI IN A LIVING ROOM

1. These chairs need to be repositioned as the corners of the fireplace will shoot "poison arrows" at people sitting in them.

2. The edges of these built-in shelves will affect anyone sitting here unless the offending edges are softened with plants.

3. A round table with a plant or lamp will move the chi on in this dark corner.

4. The corner of this pillar will send a "poison arrow" at the occupant of the chair; the chair can be moved or the edge of the pillar softened in some way.

5. Anybody who chooses to sit in this seat will be unaffected by this pillar as it is a safe distance away.

6. Uplighters in these corners of the room will lift the energy.

SLANTING WALLS

These are becoming increasingly common as expanding families in small houses convert attic space into rooms. Attic rooms with sloping ceilings are often turned into children's bedrooms or home offices. Sleeping or working under a slope depresses personal chi and these areas do nothing to aid the regenerative process of sleep nor creative processes during the day. Sloping ceilings also create a visual imbalance in a room. Mirrors and lights may help to create the illusion of lifting the slope and paint can achieve the same effect. Such rooms are far better used as hobby or play rooms or for any activity of a temporary nature.

If possible, it is preferable to have a smaller room of a conventional shape created instead of a room with sloping walls. A good solution is to fill the sloping walls in with built-in cupboards for storage. Where roof windows are installed to let light into attic conversions, make sure it is possible to see more out of them than just a patch of sky.

▼ *Placing storage cupboards under the eaves gives an attic room a more regular shape.*

BEAMS

Beams are not recommended in Feng Shui because they can be oppressive when positioned over a bed, stove or desk and suppress the chi of the people living beneath them. Proportion, however, is everything. In a barn conversion or in some of the eco-houses now being built, the ceilings are high and often vaulted so the beams do not seem to press down on the occupants. The reverse problem occurs when people and small-scale furniture rattle around in vast spaces and are unable to gather chi around them. However, beams in normally proportioned houses do tend to upset the flow of chi in a room, especially if we

▼ *The oppressive effect of these beams is reduced by painting them a light colour.*

position ourselves in unsuitable places under them. Simply by moving the dining table, desk or bed, we can often overcome any difficulties.

Many people dream of owning a country cottage, complete with roses round the door, log fires and beams. Traditionally it has been the custom to paint beams black so that they stand out, but when these cottages were built it is highly unlikely that this was their original colour. In the same way that pollution and time turn pale sandstone buildings in cities to a tobacco brown, so cooking and fires down the ages have transformed pale oak beams into charcoal-coloured wood. Interior fashions change, however, and it is now more common for beams to be painted the same colour as the ceiling,

▲ *These beams are unobtrusive because the roof is so high. Avoid sitting under the low crossbeam running across the room.*

a welcome trend which makes all the difference to low-ceilinged rooms.

Another way of reducing the effect of beams is to use uplighters underneath them, which give the illusion of "lifting" the beam. Small, light-coloured hanging objects will lighten a beam. Do not hang large, dark or heavy objects below a beam, or anything that collects dust. False ceilings can be attached to beams, either

▼ *Sloping walls and a beam across the bed make this an inauspicious bedroom. The insecurity of the window behind the bed adds to the effect.*

the conventional type or translucent ones with light behind. In larger spaces, such as restaurants, beams have been successfully mirrored, but this would not look good in most homes. Muslin or other fabrics will hide them, but these will harbour dust and create stagnant chi unless washed regularly. Traditionally, bamboo flutes tied with red ribbon were hung from the beam to create an auspicious octagon shape. Beams over a bed are believed to cause illnesses to occupants at

◄ *This modern living room is made inauspicious by the sloping walls and the dark beam running down the centre of the room.*

▲ *Imagine this room with dark beams – the light beams create quite a different effect.*

the points where they cross. A beam that runs along the length of the bed can cause a rift between the couple that shares it. When beams are situated over the stove or dining room table, they are thought to hamper the fortunes of the family. If they are over a desk, they may hinder the creative flow of the person who works there, and may even be a cause of depression. It is certainly better not to sleep under a beam, and sitting in a chair under a beam or under a gallery is not a comfortable experience either.

DOORS AND WINDOWS

Doors represent our freedom and our access to the outside world; they are also a barrier, acting as protection, supplying support and comfort. Windows act as our eyes on the world. Both play an important role in Feng Shui and if our access or vision through them is impeded in any way we may suffer problems as a consequence.

DOORS

Open doors allow us access to a room or to the outside world. Closed doors shut off a room or our entire home. If either of these functions is impeded, then the

▶ *The uplifting view from this window has not been restricted by curtains or blinds.*

chi flow around the house will suffer. Doors which squeak, stick, have broken latches, or handles too close to the edge so we scrape our knuckles whenever we open them, should all be repaired. Keep a wedge close to doors that might slam irritatingly in the breeze.

Ideally, a door should not open to a

▼ *Stained glass panels in doors permit light and lift the energy in dark spaces.*

CURES FOR PROBLEM DOORS

▲ If doors are located opposite each other, place an obstruction such as a table or a bookcase to slow down the chi.

▲ Where doors are out of alignment, create a balance by positioning mirrors or pictures on each side.

▲ Where there are three or more doors in a row, break up the perspective by hanging low lights or positioning semi-circular tables to slow down the chi.

▲ Where an opened door restricts the view into a room, position a mirror to correct this. Doors were traditionally hung in this way to prevent draughts. This practice may also have arisen because of the desire to preserve modesty in Victorian times.

restricted view of the whole room on entering, but doors in old houses used to be hung in this way to prevent draughts or, some speculate, to preserve modesty during the decorous Victorian era.

WINDOWS

Sash windows which only open halfway restrict the amount of chi that can enter a room. Some double-glazed units only open halfway, with the same result. Ideally, all windows should open fully, and outwards. Beware of windows which have fixed double-glazed panels with only a small opening section at the top. These can cause fatal accidents if fire breaks out; they are usually fitted with safety glass, so it is virtually impossible to smash them.

▲ *Adding an attractive stained-glass hanging can offer some privacy while creating a lively energy in the room.*

▼ *This stencilled decoration allows privacy in a bathroom, while at the same time letting in as much daylight as possible.*

▲ *Tied-back curtains are ideal here as they do not restrict the pleasant view.*

If these have been fitted in your home, it is advisable to remove them as soon as possible, particularly in children's rooms.

Safety is, of course, paramount in children's rooms and measures should be taken to ensure that they cannot fall out of windows.

The top of a window should be as tall as the tallest person in the house. Everyone should have a view of the sky through the seasons or they will lose their connection with the natural world. Drooping blinds which prevent this view lower the chi of a room considerably, and slatted blinds send cutting chi into the room.

If you keep your curtains closed during the day, the chances are that you are depressed and feel vulnerable. Net curtains, although necessary in some areas, blur the view out of the window. Experiment with other solutions, such as large plants, coloured glass or window stickers to prevent the outside world looking in. The aim should be to see out as much as possible. South-west-facing windows will, however, need some screening in summer, particularly in a study or kitchen.

Too many windows can create excessive yang since they blast the house with chi, while too few windows restrict its flow and are yin. Windows too near the

▲ *The seating in this room impedes access to the window, and can be easily rearranged.*

floor in attic rooms feel unstable and a solid object or low table should be placed in front. It is preferable for bathrooms to have windows with an air flow. If this is not available, a water feature containing aromatic oils should be used and an extraction unit installed.

Too many windows in the dining room are considered to be especially inauspicious since the aim is to gather chi around the dining table and the food prepared for friends and family.

▼ *This lovely etched bathroom window allows the occupants privacy, but still permits the maximum amount of light.*

MATERIALS

The materials with which we surround ourselves affect us on a physical level by how they feel and what they look like. They also affect us on a psychological level through their energy. Like everything else, materials have

▼ *A wooden floor makes the room look attractive and warm.*

▲ *Natural materials such as wood, wicker and cotton fabrics look fresh and inviting.*

elemental qualities which affect the chi of the part of the home in which they are used, and they can also have a profound effect on our health and well-being.

Hard, reflective surfaces such as those used in the kitchen have a yang energy and chi moves across them quickly. Soft materials and those with depth of colour or texture are yin and tend to slow chi movement down.

MATERIALS AND HEALTH

Our choice of materials for fabrics and soft furnishings, furniture, decorating materials, and cleaning and washing

PLANTS WHICH CLEAN THE AIR

Lady Palm – *Rhapis excelsa*
Anthurium – *Anthurium andraeanum* (below right)
Rubber Plant – *Ficus robusta*
Dwarf Banana – *Musa cavendishii*
Peace Lily – *Spathiphyllum*
Ivy – *Hedera helix*
Heart Leaf Philodendron
Croton – *Codiaeum variegatum pictum*
Kalanchoe – *Kalanchoe blossfeldiana* (below left)
Golden Pothos – *Epipremnum aureum*
Ficus alii
Boston Fern – *Nephrolepis exaltata* 'Bostoniensis'

agents can play a part in our health and well-being. Each of us takes responsibility for our own health and that of our families whenever we choose materials for use inside our homes. Many substances present in the products we select can cause life-threatening illnesses over time and many are known to be responsible for allergies.

While investigating the air quality inside spacecraft, scientists at NASA discovered that some plants are useful in extracting harmful substances from the atmosphere. This is a very good reason for introducing plants into our homes, in addition to their other virtues. The list above shows plants which have been found useful in cleaning the air.

◀ *Wicker furniture is strong and comfortable, and it is also biodegradable.*

MATERIALS AND THE FIVE ELEMENTS

Materials and their colours and shapes can be used to enhance, weaken or support the energy of an area according to the relationships of the elements.

WOOD

Wood plays a crucial role in most houses. Its strength can support the structure of a house, yet its grain suggests fluidity and movement. Highly polished woods conduct chi quickly but stripped pine seems to absorb it. Wood is ideal for use on floors as it is easy to clean and does not harbour dust and mites, which can cause allergies.

BAMBOO, WICKER AND RATTAN

These natural products fall into the Wood element category. In contrast to the yang characteristics of highly polished wood, these materials tend to be yin and thus slow down chi.

COIR, SISAL, SEA GRASS AND RUSH MATTING

These are popular because they are natural products. They make attractive floor coverings but are difficult to clean; this must be done regularly or they will harbour dirt and insects.

FABRICS

These can be made of natural fibres, like cotton and linen which belong to the Wood element, or from man-made fibres. Provided they are not treated with chemicals for fire or stain resistance, natural fibres are preferred since man-made fibres create static electricity and deplete the beneficial negative ions in the home. Fabrics can encourage stagnant chi if they become faded and dirty.

PLASTICS

Plastics and other man-made materials generally fall into the Fire element category as they have usually been produced using heat processes. They can block chi and produce harmful vapours and chemicals which may affect health, so they should be kept to a minimum.

METAL

Metal objects — steel, chrome and other metals — speed up chi flow. The reflective surfaces suggest efficiency and action, and metal is therefore useful in the kitchen and in stagnant areas such as bathrooms. Being smooth and reflective, glass is often classified in the Metal element and some of its qualities are similar.

GLASS

Glass is often classified as the Metal element and shares some of its qualities. However, glass has depth, and light reflecting on it suggests patterns which flow like Water. Sand is used in the production of glass, so sometimes it also suggests Earth. It depends on the energetic quality of the particular glass and the use to which it is put.

CLAY AND CERAMICS

These two related materials fall into the Earth element category. They can be yin or yang in nature, depending on whether or not their surfaces are shiny. Glazed surfaces such as china and vases are more yang and they conduct chi quickly.

STONE AND MARBLE

Stone floors and walls fall into the Earth element category. They tend to be yin since their surfaces are non-reflective and the natural patterning on them gives them depth. Stone floors are stable and are particularly useful in kitchens. Marble, on the other hand, is yang because it is smooth, hard and polished. The natural patterns in marble also suggest the flow of the Water element.

MIRRORS

Mirrors have been described as "the aspirin" of Feng Shui and they have many curative uses. They should always reflect something pleasant, such as an attractive view or a landscape, which will bring the vibrant energy of a garden or scene into the house. When placing a mirror to enhance a space or "cure" an area, be aware of what is reflected in it or a problem may be created elsewhere. Mirrors should never distort or cut into the image of a person as this symbolically distorts or cuts their chi. They should always have frames to contain the chi of the image.

Mirrors are useful in small spaces where they apparently double the size of the area. Don't hang them opposite a door or a window since they merely reflect the chi back at itself and do not allow it to flow around the home. Mirrors opposite each other indicate restlessness and are not recommended. Other reflective objects can be used in the same way as mirrors; for example, highly polished door furniture, metal pots, glass bowls and shiny surfaces.

▲ *This hallway is already light but the mirror makes it positively sparkle. Mirrors create an illusion of space and depth.*

▼ *A mirror will make a small space seem much larger. Do not position it directly opposite a door or window.*

IRREGULAR SPACES
Where part of a house is "missing", in other words irregularly shaped, mirrors can be used to effectively recreate the missing space and make a regular shape.

STAGNANT AREAS
Use mirrors in dark corners and at bends in passages to help the chi to circulate around these awkward places.

LONG CORRIDORS
In long corridors the chi moves too fast. Mirrors offer one method of slowing the chi down. Position several mirrors in a staggered manner to reflect pleasant images placed on the opposite wall.

MIRRORS TO DEFLECT
Convex mirrors are used in Feng Shui to deflect fast-moving chi or the influences

THE DO'S AND DON'TS OF MIRRORS

Do
- ✔ Have frames around mirrors
- ✔ Keep them clean
- ✔ Replace broken ones
- ✔ Reflect your whole image

DON'T
- ✘ Have joins or mirror tiles
- ✘ Hang mirrors opposite each other
- ✘ Place them opposite the bed
- ✘ Place them opposite doors
- ✘ Place them directly opposite windows
- ✘ Hang Bagua mirrors indoors

THE BAGUA MIRROR

The markings on the Bagua mirror are a kind of shorthand, representing the energies of the Cosmos.

of uncomfortable features outside the house, for example, corners of buildings, telegraph poles and trees which over-power the front of the house. They will also deflect unwanted influences indoors, but because they distort images position them where they will not reflect people.

BAGUA MIRRORS

Bagua mirrors are used to protect a house from malign energies which may attack the occupants. They can often be seen outside Chinese homes and shops. They are used on front doors to deflect the influences of negative energy sources – harsh corners, tall objects and other features. Bagua mirrors represent a yin energy cycle and, as such, should never be hung inside the house or they will affect the energies of the occupants.

▲ *If a house is not of a perfect shape, a mirror hung inside will symbolically reflect the missing area.*

The Wealth area of this house is missing. Place mirrors to symbolically repair the shape and energize the missing space.

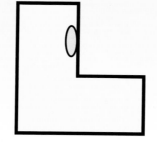

Use a mirror to repair the shape of an L-shaped room by symbolically drawing in the missing area.

A mirror placed in this gloomy corner, reflecting a view or plant, will enliven a dark space and prevent energy stagnating.

Place a mirror to reflect a bright picture on the opposite wall and thus bring energy to this dark area.

A mirror in this position will not allow the chi into the house or room and will reflect it back through the door.

This is a better position as it draws the chi into and through the living area and does not act as a barrier.

PLANTS

Plants play an important role in Feng Shui because they bring a life force into the home and help to keep the air fresh. Depending on their shape, plants create different types of energy. Upright plants with pointed leaves are yang, and are useful in the south and in corners to move energy. Round-leaved and drooping plants are more yin and calming, and best placed in the north. Plants should be healthy – sick plants and those which shed leaves and flowers profusely will create stagnant energy.

COLOUR AND SHAPE

Plants with shapes and colours that correspond to the Five Elements are ideal. Care should be taken when siting spiky plants to ensure that they are not directing harmful energy towards a chair where someone may sit.

INDOOR BULBS

SPRING: Dwarf tulip, Dwarf narcissus, Crocus, Hyacinth (above)

SUMMER: *Scilla peruviana*, *Albuca humulis*, *Calochortus subalpinus*, *Rocoea humeana*

AUTUMN: Nerine, Autumn crocus, Cyclamen, *Liriope muscari*

WINTER: *Iris reticulata*, *Chionodoxa luciliae*, Muscari, Cymbidium

▲ *Colourful plants will brighten any area and increase Wood energy. Plants in these colours will benefit an Earth area.*

▲ *The money plant has been adopted as the Feng Shui plant. Its leaves resemble coins and Metal energy.*

▶ *This trained ivy plant brings a lively energy to a room. It would look best in the west or north-west.*

PLANTS THAT REPRESENT THE FIVE ELEMENTS

▲ *Geraniums are easy to grow on a sunny windowsill and represent Fire.*

FIRE: Geranium, Cordyline, Begonia, Bromeliad, Poinsettia, Aspidistra.
EARTH: Slipper flower, Marigolds, Sunflowers and other yellow plants.
METAL: Money plant, Jasmine, Fittonia, Oleander, Calathea.

▲ *All the elements are here, captured in both the colours and the shapes of this attractive pot of lillies.*

▲ *Summer jasmine is often grown in an arch shape. Its delicate white flowers have a beautiful scent.*

WATER: The Water element can be introduced by standing plant pots on blue or clear glass nuggets.
WOOD: All plants are representative of the Wood element.

FLOWERS

Flowers look beautiful in a vase but, once cut, they are technically dead and often stand forgotten in stagnant water. The cut-flower industry uses vast amounts of energy in heating greenhouses, transportation and the manufacture of chemicals to feed their products and keep them pest-free. Choose potted plants instead. You could grow pots of bulbs through the seasons and plant them afterwards in the garden.

Dried flowers are also technically dead and have a stagnant energy, particularly when their colours fade and they gather dust. As an alternative, pictures of flowers, brightly painted wooden replicas and silk flowers are all acceptable to symbolize growth and stimulate energy in the house.

THE FENG SHUI PLANT

The money plant (*Crassula ovata*) has been adopted as the Feng Shui plant. The name helps, but the round succulent leaves are representative of Metal energy. Use them in the west and north-west. If used in the south-east (the Wealth area), their Metal energy will be in conflict with the Wood energy of that direction.

▼ *Use a pretty flowering plant in the house like this Cymbidium, instead of cut flowers.*

▶ *This bright arrangement would do well in the south-west – an Earth area.*

USE PLANTS TO:

◆ Hide a jutting corner
◆ Move energy in a recessed corner
◆ Harmonize Fire and Water energy in kitchens
◆ Slow down chi in corridors
◆ Drain excess Water energy in the bathroom
◆ Bring life into the house
◆ Enhance the east and south-east, and support the south

LIGHTING

L ife on Earth depends directly or indirectly on the sun. Our bodies are attuned to its cycles and in every culture the daily rhythms of light and dark are built into the mythology. In China, the yin-yang or T'ai Chi symbol reflects the daily and annual cycles of the sun: the white yang side representing daytime and

▲ *Our bodies need plenty of sunlight in order to stay healthy.*

▶ *Muslin filters the light in rooms where the sun's glare is too strong, or offers privacy.*

▼ *Stained glass is very decorative and provides privacy in a room which is overlooked.*

the dark yin side night-time. In the modern world, many of us spend a lot of time inside buildings and our rhythms become out-of-tune with the natural cycle of the sun. In northern countries, which have little sunlight, a condition known as SAD (Seasonal Affective Disorder) is prevalent. It is treated with light that imitates the ultraviolet and infra-red rays of the sun.

The correct type and level of light are very important to our general health and well-being. In our homes, natural light is important but its quality varies throughout the day according to the way our houses face. Natural light can cause glare or create shadows and we often have to subdue it or enhance it by artificial means. Light can be reflected off shiny surfaces or filtered by net or muslin curtains, blinds or frosted or tinted glass. Being aware of how natural light comes into our homes enables us to position our furniture and arrange our activities to make the best use of it.

ARTIFICIAL LIGHTING

In rooms where we are active, such as kitchens, offices and workrooms, and where safety is important, for example on staircases, direct lighting is necessary. In rooms we relax in – living rooms and bedrooms – we can use softer lighting which can be reflected or diffused. To highlight particular areas, such as a picture, chopping board or desk, task lighting can be used.

The position of lighting has a profound effect on the occupants of a house. If shadows are cast where we read or prepare food, or the lights flicker, or light glares on to the computer or TV screen, we will constantly be irritated. Harsh lighting can also affect our moods.

The quality of light is important. Ordinary light bulbs produce light which veers towards the red end of the spectrum, with little blue or green light. Fluorescent light is the opposite; it emits higher electromagnetic fields than other sources and its flicker can cause headaches. Full spectrum lighting was designed to copy natural daylight as much as possible, but unfortunately contains slightly higher levels of ultraviolet radiation than ordinary light sources.

Energy production is a drain on the world's natural resources. Recent developments designed to reduce this include CFL (compact fluorescent lamp) bulbs, which not only last longer but also use

▼ *Soft wall lighting helps us to relax at the end of a stressful day.*

▲ *Glass bricks have been used here instead of a solid wall. They can be very useful if you want to open up dark areas.*

► *Use uplighters to transform dark corners. Placed under heavy beams, they serve to lighten their negative effect.*

less electricity. Tungsten-halogen lamps give a bright, white light that is close to daylight. The high-voltage varieties are too bright for task lighting but are useful as uplighters; the low-voltage varieties can be used for spotlights. These bulbs are also energy-efficient.

ELECTROSTRESS

We are becoming increasingly aware of the negative effects of electromagnetic radiation on the human body. The effects of exposure to ionizing radiation in X-rays and ultraviolet rays in sunlight are now well-known. The low-frequency radiation which surrounds power lines has also been linked to childhood illness. Such radiation also exists around electrical appliances. Non-ionizing radiation emitted by household appliances can be equally harmful over time. Cathode ray tubes in televisions and computer monitors are particularly harmful because both adults and children now spend so much time in front of them. It is wise to sit as far away as possible from the screen. Lap-top computers should not be used on our laps as we would then be connected to an electric circuit. The electromagnetic field around ionizers has a particularly large range so it is not a good idea to place them in bedrooms.

▲ *Placing a Boston fern next to the television screen has been shown to absorb some of the radiation it emits.*

◄ *Round-the-clock working and satellite links to the rest of the world have resulted in Hong Kong having higher-than-average electromagnetic activity.*

▼ *Mobile phones are convenient and allow us to conduct business outside, but pose a health risk if used constantly. A laptop computer should not be used on our laps.*

◀ Microwave ovens can damage your health if they leak. Have them checked annually as you would other household fixtures. They are not well regarded in Feng Shui.

▶ A gadget-free bedroom is essential for a healthy body and peace of mind. While we sleep, our body cells can regenerate naturally, a process which works best if unimpeded by any harmful external influences.

We live in an electrical "soup". Radio, TV and microwave emissions pass around and through us wherever we live. There are few places left on Earth where this is not the case. Satellites connect continents instantly and we can communicate with people across the world, but at a price. Recent research into the use of mobile telephones indicates that frequent use can affect us. The radiation from the appliances we use every day of our lives has been linked to various cancers, allergies, Parkinson's disease, Alzheimer's disease, cataracts, ME and even the total breakdown of the immune system.

Despite our awareness of the effects of radiation, we are so dependent on appliances and communication technology that we are unwilling, or unable, to live without them. We should therefore take precautions. At night, electric blankets should never be left on when we are in bed; if we must use them, they should be unplugged from the mains before we get into bed. Water beds are connected to the electricity supply, so in Feng Shui terms they display the conflict of Fire (electricity) and Water. We need to feel secure when we sleep and the constant motion of a water bed is not a natural way for us to rest.

Microwave ovens are potentially the most dangerous of all household appliances and should be used with care. They have been found to emit low-frequency radiation far in excess of that known to cause lymphatic cancer in children.

Apartments that have under-floor or overhead heating systems should be avoided as they can create the effect of living in an electromagnetic box.

PRECAUTIONS

- ◆ Use mobile phones as little as possible
- ◆ Make lengthy social calls from a conventional telephone
- ◆ Fit screen filters to VDUs
- ◆ Sit, and make sure children sit, at least 2 m (6 ft) away from the television
- ◆ Sit as far away from the computer as possible when not working
- ◆ Limit children's use of the computer
- ◆ Do not use the computer and television as substitute babysitters
- ◆ Do not stand near a microwave when it is on
- ◆ Dry your hair naturally instead of using electrical appliances
- ◆ Choose gas or wood-burning stoves and heaters rather than electric
- ◆ Keep all electrical appliances away from the bed
- ◆ Do not have wiring under the bed
- ◆ Do not use storage heaters in bedrooms

▲ Children sleep better if they are not surrounded by stimulating equipment.

▼ A wood-burning stove lends an attractive focus to a room.

▼ Storing electrical equipment out of sight will help us to relax.

THE SENSES: SIGHT

What we see affects us positively or negatively, or even subconsciously so we may not even be aware of the effect. If we surround ourselves with wonderful views, bright colours, interesting food and a clean and clear environment we are more likely to lead full and happy lives, because our surroundings will reflect a positive attitude to life. The reverse is equally true.

Most homes have problem areas – dark corners which would benefit from light, rooms with columns or L-shaped rooms where the corners point at us – but we can disguise them with plants and materials to soften the edges. There may be things outside which affect us and we may want to keep their influence out.

▲ *Skyscapes are so beautiful that we should make sure we can capture a view of them in our homes.*

We can attempt to deflect the problem with mirrors and other reflective objects, or create a barrier, such as a hedge or shrub, to keep it at bay. There is a difference between this type of positive, or yang, barrier designed to keep the negative exterior forces out and a yin barrier which we sometimes create to keep our own negative energies in – tall hedges and walls and drawn curtains. Wherever the ancient Chinese had a wall, there would be a window, or "Moon Gate", in it through which to see the world beyond and open up future possibilities.

◄ *"Moon Gates" were built into ancient walls in China to afford a glimpse of the world outside.*

▲ *This intricately decorated window can be found in a temple in China.*

▼ *Crystals are used to bring a sparkle to stuck energy. Suspend one in a window and the light will shine through it, creating a rainbow effect on a wall or ceiling.*

CRYSTALS

Colour resonates with us on both a conscious and a subconscious level, and can affect our moods. The combination of crystal and light gives a lively dancing pattern which will enliven a dark room if the crystal is hung in a window. Where energy is stuck, crystals can help to move it on.

Crystals should be used with care. They have many facets which break light up into tiny segments and can do the same to other energies. If the energy of an area is not working, do not hang up a crystal to repair it – or the problem will be exacerbated. A small crystal is adequate for the average home, but larger ones would be needed for a large area.

▶ *Coloured glass panels in a window add life to a colourless room. They also provide privacy and so are ideal for a bathroom or for ground floor rooms.*

▼ *This lovely room has been transformed by the balanced pairs of stained glass windows. Little extra decoration is needed.*

COLOURED GLASS

Coloured glass makes a bolder statement than crystal and its effects can be stunning. Many urban houses have side doors which look out on to a wall and there is a temptation, if they are overlooked by a window from a neighbouring house, to keep a blind permanently down. Replacing the plain glass in a door or window with bold coloured glass which supports the elements of the area will bring a wonderful energy into a dark room and transform it. Stained glass is especially decorative and suitable for most rooms in the home.

SIGHT ENHANCERS

Natural light, Lamps,
Candles, Glass and crystal, Colour,
Still water, Moon Gates,
Reflective metals,
Windows, Mirrors

THE SENSES: SOUND

Each of the Five Elements governs a different musical quality and sound. We all connect to a particular sound and in Chinese medicine the tone of our voice is categorized according to the elements and used in diagnosis. We each have our own favourite sounds. Gentle background music, the rustle of leaves, bird songs – all have a therapeutic effect. Where noise is rhythmic – a dripping tap, music from a neighbour's party, even someone sneezing at regular intervals – it can grate on our nerves.

Pleasant sounds in the right place and at the right time can soothe and refresh. Bubbling water will create a peaceful ambience and slow us down. If we want to bring life to a place, honky-tonk music, drums and cymbals will fulfil the purpose. Background sounds are comforting and the sound of passing traffic or a ticking clock can be reassuring.

WIND CHIMES

Wind chimes feature in Feng Shui as an enhancer and it is interesting to note how people respond differently to their

▼ *The vibrations from Tibetan bells will energize a room.*

various tones. Take care when using wind chimes near fences since your neighbours may not enjoy their sound as much as you do.

Wind chimes are used to slow energy down, for example, where a staircase faces the front door, but only if they are activated as the door opens. Chimes are also used in the kitchen where people stand at the sink or stove with their backs to the door, because it is comforting to know that the chimes will sound if anyone enters.

Chimes should be hollow to allow the chi in. They can be used to enhance the Metal area of a building, particularly if placed outside the door of a west-facing house, until 2003, when they should be removed. Do not use them in a Wood area (east or south-east) because in that position they are detrimental to the energy of the area.

▼ *The deep-toned, soothing ticking of a grandfather clock is a reassuring sound.*

▲ *Here wind chimes help to balance the negative effect of a sloping ceiling.*

WATER

The sound of gently bubbling water can be relaxing and there are many delightful indoor water features available. Water should be placed in the north, the east, where it is particularly auspicious until 2003, and in the south-east. From 2004 until 2023, the south-west is auspicious. Fish tanks are recommended, but must be clean, and contain living plants and natural features. Neglected tanks and unhealthy fish will have a negative effect. The preferred number of fish is nine, one being black to absorb negative chi.

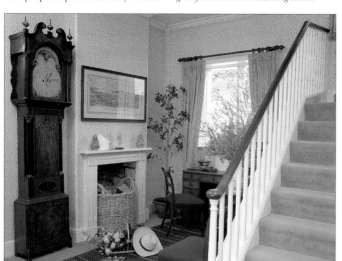

> **SOUND ENHANCERS**
>
> Wind chimes, Moving water, Music, Clocks, Rustling leaves

THE SENSES: TOUCH

Too often disregarded, touch is as vital as the other senses and is linked to our primeval desire to be in contact with the Earth. No mother can forget her first contact with a new baby – skin on skin is the most basic yet the most magical feeling there is. The tactile sensations in our homes affect our feelings of comfort and security. A scratchy plant that brushes our ankles as we return home will colour our evening, and a cold or harsh feel underfoot as we step out of bed affects the start of our day.

People who have impaired vision develop their other senses and touch becomes much more important. Guide dogs provide physical contact as well as being their owner's eyes. Isolated elderly people are said to live longer if they have pets to stroke.

When we are depressed, physical contact such as a hug from a relative or partner plays an important part in the healing process. Those who are deprived of physical affection as children often have difficulty making relationships.

▲ *No mother ever forgets her first skin-to-skin contact with her new baby.*

The materials with which we surround ourselves in our homes make a considerable impact on us. Few people can resist the urge to stroke a beautiful wooden bowl, although they might pass by a steel sculpture without touching it. Visitors to stately homes are asked to refrain from stroking fabrics and priceless furniture, but it is an irresistible urge, especially if the furnishings are particularly sumptuous. If we clothe ourselves and cover our furniture in fabrics which feel soft and luxurious, it will positively affect the way we feel. The yin-yang balance in our homes is revealed in the sense of touch. Yang rooms like the kitchen and study are full of yang metal objects which are utilitarian, we would never dream of connecting with these except on a working basis. In yin rooms (bedrooms and other rooms for relaxation) we put on warm and comfortable clothing and snuggle into soft beds and sofas.

▲ *Velvet furnishings and accessories feel wonderfully luxurious.*

◄ *Different textures provide sensual appeal and give a room character.*

TOUCH ENHANCERS

Plants, Wooden objects, Fabrics, Pets, People, Fruit, Smooth objects

THE SENSES: TASTE

This is not as easy as the other senses to describe in terms of Feng Shui yet it forms as great a part of our well-being as any sense. The Chinese see the tastes affiliated to the Five Elements as an integral part of life. If we are to change our perceptions and lifestyles, part of the process includes how we treat our bodies. If the chi is to flow unblocked, then we need to live in a holistic way in every aspect of our lives.

"We are what we eat" expresses the view that our diet directly affects our health. The frantic lifestyles that many of us lead mean that we often grab what we can to eat without taking balance into account. Modern medicine may come up with the cures, but if we eat healthy balanced diets then we are less likely to become ill in the first place.

▲ *Spend time preparing home-cooked meals rather than resorting to store-bought foods.*

Using yin and yang and the Five Elements in the kitchen is a science in itself. Chinese herbal medicine balances the constitution using the same techniques as Feng Shui does to balance an environment. (Chaucer's red-faced, lecherous Summoner in *The Canterbury Tales*, a lover of onions and leeks, is a classic case of an excess of the Fire element.) Being aware of the balance of elements in our food, and of the nutritional value

◄ *Using fresh natural ingredients keeps us healthy – and tastes wonderful.*

of the man-made fast food products which we now consume, enables us to take charge of all aspects of our lives. The benefits and disadvantages of genetically engineered food products are currently being debated, but we do not need scientific reports to tell us that we should make time in our lives to use natural ingredients and not rely on packaged food when we do not know the effects of the chemicals they contain.

SUPPORTIVE FOODS

Once we have consulted the "Chinese Animals" Table and discovered which element governs our sign, we can see below which food types support us. Using "The Relationships of the Five Elements" table, we will then be able to see which of the elements are beneficial to us and which are not, and adjust our eating habits accordingly.

Wood	sour
Fire	bitter
Earth	sweet
Metal	pungent
Water	salt

THE SENSES: SMELL

Large stores know only too well the power of the sense of smell. Who can fail to be tempted by the aroma of freshly baked bread at the supermarket entrance, pumped through grills to lure us into the store where the bakery is almost always in the farthest corner?

Animals excrete pheromones to attract their mates and to mark their territory. Our homes also have a unique smell and most of us, if blindfolded, could tell which of our friends' homes we were entering. First impressions make an

▲ *The smell of freshly-baked bread and natural foods heighten our senses.*

▲ *A herb path by the back door will smell wonderful and give us pleasure.*

▼ *Scented oils give pleasant aromas and can make a colour statement too.*

impact and if our homes smell less than fresh, this can affect how comfortable we and our visitors feel there.

There is something very different about the subtle smell of lavender as we brush past it in the garden on a warm evening after rain and the artificial lavender-scented air-fresheners sold commercially. Natural smells affect us in a way that manufactured scents never can, with the added advantage of not causing us respiratory problems or polluting the atmosphere. There is nothing to beat the flower-perfumed fresh air which wafts through an open window from a garden, balcony or window box. Many cultures use incense to sweeten the air, and we are now beginning to rediscover the long-lost knowledge of the benefits to health of certain aromatic oils.

SMELL ENHANCERS
Fresh air, Aromatic oils, Plants, Fresh potpourri, Fruit

COLOUR

The Tao teaches that out of the interplay of yin and yang all things come. Yin is the blackness which absorbs all colours and yang the whiteness which reflects them. They give rise to the Five Elements and their associated colour representations, from which arise the whole spectrum of colours. Colour is vibration and we each respond to it on many levels, consciously and unconsciously. Colour affects how comfortable we are in different environments and can affect our moods. Our use of colour also affects how others perceive us. Colour is used to cure physical ailments and can be used symbolically to enhance spaces or evoke emotions.

When we use colour we are also working with light since light contains all colours, each with its own frequency. Every situation is different – each home

▲ *This room works wonderfully well. All the elements are there but not contrived.*

▼ *African colours – browns, beiges and terracottas – predominate here.*

BEWARE PEACH

Using the colour peach in your bedroom is asking for trouble if you are married. "Peach-Blossom Luck" is a well-known concept in China, meaning a husband or wife with a roving eye. A married person may be drawn into adultery. A single person, however, will have an active social life but will probably be unable to find a life partner.

and each room within it. The light quality depends on the aspect, the size of the windows and how they are decorated, artificial light sources and the size of the rooms. The materials we use on floors and in decorations and furnishings have the ability to reflect and transmit light or to absorb it. We can use colour to create illusions – of size (dark colours absorb more light than lighter ones); of depth (natural pigments draw light in or reflect it according to the time of day and the season); and of movement (spots of colour around a room create movement and energy there).

Light quality varies around the world. In Africa, pigments, fabrics and skins in browns, beiges and terracottas are used where the sun beats down under a bright blue sky. In Britain, where the climate suggests an indoor life and the light is much less vibrant, the same colours signify closing in and, used to excess, can

lead to withdrawal and depression. Similarly, the intense colours of Indian silks and the warm colours of the Mediterranean palette have to be used with care when introduced in countries where light quality differs. However, they can play a useful role in moving the energy and, with thought, can be effective.

▼ *Mediterranean colours make us think of sunshine and holidays.*

◀ In this conservatory, the Metal and Wood elements are in conflict.

▶ The colours green (Wood), red (Fire) and yellow (Earth) balance the Five Elements.

THE FIVE ELEMENTS

The five colours associated with the elements evoke the quality of the energy of each one. We use them to highlight areas of our lives we wish to concentrate on, and the Bagua diagram gives us the associated colours for each direction. In Feng

Shui balance and harmony are essential. We should decorate our homes according to our tastes or we will never be comfortable there. We should remember the purpose of the room and the element associated with the direction it is in. Then we can achieve true balance and harmony. It would be treating the subject superficially to ensure that a room has, say, a cushion in each of the Five Elemental colours, but a single green-stemmed red artificial tulip in a glass vase in the south of an all-white room would bring in the Wood element in the green

stem, and the Fire element in the red flower. The Metal element is represented by the white room, the Water element by the light moving through the glass vase and the Earth element in the sand used to make the glass and as the medium which gave rise to the flower.

THE COLOURS

White represents a fresh canvas and black symbolizes a clean slate upon which we can create a picture with the colours below, as well as the many shades and hues which evolve from them.

RED: Red is stimulating and dominant, it reduces the size of rooms and increases the size of objects. It is useful as an accent colour. It is not suitable for dining rooms, children's bedrooms, kitchens or workshops. It is associated with warmth, prosperity and stimulation, but also anger, shame and hatred.

YELLOW: Yellow is associated with enlightenment and intellect, it stimulates the brain and aids digestion. Its positive qualities are optimism, reason and decisiveness, while its negative are craftiness, exaggeration and rigidity. Suitable for hallways and kitchens, but not for meditation rooms or bathrooms.

GREEN: Green symbolizes growth, fertility and harmony; it is restful and refreshing. Its positive associations are optimism, freedom and balance, and its negatives envy and deceit. Good in therapy rooms, conservatories and bathrooms but not in family rooms, playrooms or studies.

BLUE: Blue is peaceful and soothing and is linked with spirituality, contemplation, mystery and patience. Its positive associations are trust, faithfulness and stability. Negatives are suspicion and melancholia. Blue can be used in meditation rooms, bedrooms, therapy rooms and as a means of enlarging spaces, but not in family rooms, dining rooms and studies.

PURPLE: Encouraging vitality, purple is impressive, dignified and spiritual. Positive associations are excitement, passion and motivation, negatives are mournfulness and force. Use in bedrooms and meditation rooms but not bathrooms or kitchens.

PINK: Pink is linked with purity of thought and has the positive association of happiness and romance with no negatives. Suitable for bedrooms but not kitchens or bathrooms.

ORANGE: A powerful and cheerful colour, orange encourages communication. Its positive qualities are happiness, concentration and intellect, and its negative is rebelliousness. Use in living or dining rooms and hallways, but not in small rooms or bedrooms.

BROWN: Brown suggests stability and weight. Its positives are safety and elegance, while its negatives are dinginess, depression and aging. Good for studies but not for bedrooms.

WHITE: White symbolizes new beginnings, purity and innocence. its positive qualities are cleanliness and freshness, its negatives cold, lifelessness, starkness. Use for bathrooms and kitchens, not suitable for children's rooms and dining rooms.

BLACK: Black is mysterious and independent. Its positive qualities are intrigue, strength and allure, while its negatives are death, darkness and evil. Often used in teenagers' rooms and in bedrooms, it should not be used in young children's rooms, therapy rooms, studies or living rooms.

CLUTTER

Clutter is a state of mind. It can be the things we haven't done which prey on our minds, like unreturned telephone calls and appointments not made, or the ideas and perceptions we hoard which prevent us from doing the things we really want to do. Everything we do not use or wear, or which we are keeping in case it comes in handy one day, constitutes clutter. Inherited objects, and those given to us as presents which we do not like but feel guilty about parting with, are also clutter.

For one reason or another, perhaps due to our upbringing or past experiences, or because we doubt our own abilities, we hang on to situations and ideas which do not let us move on. We may stay in a job thinking we are indis-

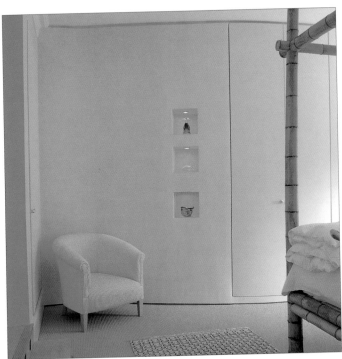

▲ *Any extraneous objects would look out of place in this cool, clutter-free bedroom, a perfect place to unwind.*

▲ *This low-beamed cottage room looks oppressive with fussy decoration and too many ornaments.*

▼ *A similar room but less cluttered gives a lighter, more airy feel.*

pensable or we are doing it out of a sense of loyalty, but often it is because we are afraid to take the leap and change direction. We may stay in a relationship through fear of emotional upheaval, or not accept a job away from a familiar area through fear of the unknown. All these attitudes clutter our thought processes but by clearing out our physical clutter we see the benefits of "letting go", which will help us to clear out the mental clutter restricting our development.

CLEARING OUT

"Things" constitute a major problem in most homes. Useless kitchen gadgets, empty gift boxes to recycle, presents we hate or have outgrown, inherited objects which fear of embarrassment or guilt will not let us part with, and an endless list of other items. We do not need these things in our lives if we are to open up and let

new experiences in. Give them to charity shops or sell them at car-boot sales and buy something you really want.

Most of us hold on to clothes "in case" we might need them, grow back into them or our children might like them one day. It is far better to live for today and create space for something new which we will enjoy wearing now.

Books are difficult to get rid of as many people believe it is a sacrilege to throw them out. If books sit and gather dust for years on end, unread and not referred to, they too constitute clutter and stuck energy and we should move them on. The world is changing fast and information becomes out of date almost before it is in print. Should we require a

▲ *If these overladen shelves are thinned out, there will be room for new books.*

can always extract any information we require from magazines provided we file it immediately in a place where we are likely to find it again.

Clutter represents stagnant energy and the list is endless – blown light bulbs we keep forgetting to replace, dead wasps and dropped leaves on the window ledge, scum marks round the bath, the unfilled vinegar shaker, the squeaking door. Each of these requires only one minute's attention, but their accumulated effect can make years of difference to the pace and quality of our lives.

Do not attempt to rid the whole house of clutter in one go. Start in a small way with a drawer, and complete the whole task of clearing out, tidying and getting rid of unwanted items before moving on to the next.

fact in ten years' time, the information will always be available elsewhere. Magazines and newspapers also constitute clutter. We are unlikely to read last week's, or even yesterday's, paper and we

▲ *There is no clutter here but enough objects and colours to make the space interesting.*

ENERGIZING OUR HOMES

When we move into a new house, or have had an unpleasant experience in our home, the energy there can become stuck and feel heavy. We can lighten it to some extent by clearing out all the clutter and by cleaning everywhere thoroughly.

Vibrations are important and we resonate at a level which is in harmony with the natural vibrations of the Earth. The senses also work at a vibrational level and if we can improve their quality in our homes we will feel the benefit. Often the vibrations which have caused

▼ *Candles represent Fire. Use with care in the South and to support the West.*

▲ *Burning aromatic oils or incense raises the energy in a room.*

every room (check first that the neighbours are out). Bells, gongs and clapping are all useful in raising the vibrational level. Take particular care to go into the corners, where energy is likely to have become stuck. Natural light should be present in the form of sunlight and candles, placed in the four corners of the room and in the centre. Smell can be introduced in the form of incense or aromatic oils. Spring water, charged by the vibrations of the moon, can be sprayed around to introduce negative ions back into the air.

▼ *Candles in the corners and centre of a room will help move any stuck energy.*

the previous owner to behave in a certain way or adopt a certain way of life will have the same effect on us and we should take note of any problems which have befallen them before moving to a new home.

There are various methods we can use to improve the vibrations in our homes. Having cleaned and rid the house of clutter, open the windows and make a noise in

USING THE SYMBOLIC BAGUA

We all wish at certain times in our lives that some aspect was working better. By focusing on a particular aspect of our lives, we can often stimulate the energy to make things work well for us. Used as a template that we can place on the plans of our home, the Symbolic Bagua gives us a tool for focus with its division into eight life sections. The eight life sections of the Bagua are: Career, Relationships, Family, Wealth, Helpful People, Children, Knowledge and Fame and each area has its own enhancers. By using some of the methods described on the following pages we can hopefully harness some of the "magic" of Feng Shui for ourselves.

The enhancements used in Feng Shui are designed to focus the mind. For example, we can create the belief that it is possible to stabilize something in our lives by using heavy objects such as stones or pictures of mountains. We can move on a "stuck" situation by creating or alluding to movement, for instance, using water or wind-blown items. Whatever image we use must have meaning for us in that we can see it physically and relate to its symbolism. Thus we should use images from our own cultures and experiences. Whatever we use, it should not clash with the element of the direction but if possible should strengthen it.

CAREER

This concerns itself with where we are going in life, either in our jobs or in our journeys through life. It can also mark the beginning of a project. ENHANCERS INCLUDE: moving images, a photograph of an aspiration such as a university, or a company brochure if applying for a job.

RELATIONSHIPS

These play an important part in our lives. Getting on well with people and having the support of partners, family or friends play a major role in a happy life.

▲ *A perfect arrangement for a table in the Relationships area of a room.*

ENHANCERS INCLUDE: double images for romance, two vases or candlesticks, a photograph of yourself with your partner or group images of friends, a poster or photograph, or a collection of something. Plants are useful to improve the chi, and ribbons or wind-activated objects will energize it as they move, provided there is a breeze. Do not use them if there is no breeze.

FAMILY

Our families, past as well as present, will have coloured who we are, how we relate to the world around us and will have

▼ *Framed photographs can be placed in the Family area of a room.*

contributed to our health and well-being. ENHANCERS INCLUDE: Family photographs and documents, and heirlooms.

WEALTH

This is often taken to be monetary wealth, but it also covers the richness of our lives, fulfilment and the accumulation of beneficial energies around us. ENHANCERS INCLUDE: coins, plants, empty bowls and movement, for example, an indoor water feature.

▲ *Chinese coins for the Wealth area – the circle symbolizes Heaven, the square Earth.*

HELPFUL PEOPLE

Interaction with others is an essential part of life, and this area is a very important one. "What goes round, comes round" and "You reap what you sow" are Eastern and Western ways of saying the same thing. If you are willing to help others and need some help in return, this is the area to focus on. ENHANCERS INCLUDE: telephones and telephone directories, and business cards.

CHILDREN

Not quite the same as family, since children are the future rather than part of the past. This area also covers personal projects – the tasks and jobs you nurture from their conception to their conclusion. ENHANCERS INCLUDE: photographs of children, project details, and your artistic and other achievements.

▲ *Family photographs of children are placed in the Children area.*

KNOWLEDGE

This is the area for wisdom and education, not of the enforced variety, but that which is sought after and which can enrich our lives. ENHANCERS INCLUDE: books, framed words of wisdom and pictures of mentors.

FAME

This does not mean notoriety for its own sake, but recognition of an undertaking well done and a sense of fulfilment.

HOME ENHANCER

An enhancer for any space that will nurture the supportive energy in any home is a feature which represents all five elements. Fill a glass or crystal bowl (Earth) with blue glass nuggets (Earth and Water), top up with water and a floating candle (Fire) and some flowers or petals (Wood). Add coins (Metal) to complete the cycle.

THE POWER OF FENG SHUI

Feng Shui works in mysterious ways and the results of any action taken may not be quite as expected. Our actions trigger the energy required to achieve the outcomes we seek. This may not correspond to what we think we need or offer a quick fix. A consultant will offer solutions having ensured that everything is balanced. If we decide to undertake some of the recommendations and not others there will be no balance. Proceed carefully. Instigate one change at a time and give it several days before introducing the next.

The following case study illustrates the unpredictable nature of Feng Shui. Richard and Anne had lived in their house for ten years and had never settled. Through lethargy they had let it run down and now could not sell it. The electric lights blew regularly and there was evidence of a water leak outside the house. The only decorating they had done was to paint the living room walls a deep pink which, together with the red carpet laid throughout the house, resulted in an overload of Fire energy.

Richard and Anne did not want to spend money on a new carpet, so they were advised to paint the walls white to drain the Fire. They had already installed a large fish tank in the Wealth area since they wanted their money to move. They put several recommendations into practice, but not the major one – the walls. The result was that the energies took over. Within a week, the washing machine flooded the ground floor, ruining the carpet and forcing out the Fire energy, the overloaded electrical system finally blew and the fish in the tank died. The Chinese use fish as a sacrifice to human bad luck, believing they soak it up on behalf of the people.

Thus Feng Shui achieved its objectives and moved the energy on. Richard and Anne were left with no choice but to fix the electrics and change the carpet, and this time they chose wisely. The changes made the house sellable and they were able to move. Never underestimate the power of Feng Shui, be prepared for the unexpected.

ENHANCERS INCLUDE: certificates, newspaper cuttings, products of achievement.

Feng Shui cannot help you to win the lottery but if you have worked hard and followed an honest and ethical path towards self-fulfilment, then the magic may work for you. If this happens, you will probably not want to win the lottery anyway and other, more rewarding bounty may come your way.

THE CENTRE OF THE BAGUA

The centre is a special place. In a house it is where the occupants meet and where the energies accumulate and flow on. It should be treated well, be bright and welcoming, and not be cluttered. Do not introduce a light fitting with five bulbs here; glass and crystal light fittings will stimulate the area far better. A round rug often works well.

THE RIGHT TIME

Most of us will have heard or read of people who have used Feng Shui and received rewards – a job, a long-awaited child, or a partner. We may be tempted to take Feng Shui on board and tweak every area of our homes in order to achieve perfection. Life is not perfect, however, and it is constantly changing. Essentially, the energies of the various directions change over time. Thus if we activate a particular area when the energies are good, things will be fine. If we leave whatever we have done when the energies are inauspicious, then we will create problems.

The adage, "If it ain't broke, don't fix it" applies. Remember when using these symbolic measures that the compass directions and their related elements are still important.

INVESTIGATING YOUR HOME

The following Feng Shui case study can only offer a glimpse into the kind of analysis which takes place when investigating a home.

William and Julia and their son Steven moved into their apartment a year ago. Julia feels comfortable there but William and Steven do not, and Steven has gradually become very run down and cannot concentrate on his schoolwork. William does some freelance work at home to supplement his income, but has not been getting many clients lately. There is tension and the couple's relationship is suffering. A Feng Shui consultant investigates the birthday of each person, their animal, the corresponding element and the compatibility of the animals.

William is a Fire – Rooster, Julia is a Metal + Rat and Steven a Water – Pig. This indicates that while William and Julia have a workable relationship with Steven, William and Julia's relationship can be difficult. According to the Five Elements relationships, Fire (William) is weakened by Metal (Julia), who in turn is weakened by Water (Steven). Being a Metal Rat with yang characteristics, Julia is quite strong and domineering so can hold her own. As a Fire Rooster, William can be inflexible and is not easily swayed by others' emotions so may not be sym-

▲ *The position of the bed is crucial. It should be protected behind and face an auspicious direction for the occupants.*

pathetic to Steven. Fortunately, as a Water Pig, Steven accepts that things are difficult and is perceptive enough to steer clear when necessary.

Next, the consultant looked at the magic numbers, the corresponding east and west directions, each person's favourable and unfavourable directions, and the compass direction of the house.

William is a 7 and belongs to the west group. Julia, a 4, belongs to the east group and Steven, an 8, belongs to the west group. The house faces south-east, an east group direction, and is therefore most supportive of Julia. William's best direction is north-west, which is missing from the house. His office falls between the south and south-west sectors. The south-west is his second-best direction and the south his sixth. Steven's room has geopathic stress by the head of his bed. His best direction is south-west and his second is north-west. Julia's best direction is north and the second south. The consultant then looked at the shape of the house, Steven's room, William's desk position and William and Julia's bed. He made recommendations listed below.

▼ *This bed is well balanced by the matching tables and lamps on either side.*

KEY TO DIAGRAM

1. A mirror here symbolically completes the house shape and seemingly draws in the energy of the missing section. A metal frame is used which represents the element of the area.

2. The head of the bed was re-positioned to face south-west, Steven's best direction, and to remove him from the stressed area.

3. Steven's desk now faces north-west, his second-best direction. This also enables him to see the door and protects him from the fast-moving chi along the long passage. The bookcase, aided by the plant on top, also protects him from the chi in the passage.

4. Semi-circular tables with silk flowers slow the chi further. The passage was too dark for live plants.

5. William's desk now faces north-west, his best position. A plant behind him prevents stagnant energy from building up in the corner. A plant on the desk

deflects fast-moving chi through the door and hides the point which would symbolically stab him as he enters.

6. The "mouth of chi" to the stove, the point of entry of the energy source and symbolic of wealth, comes from the south, Julia's second-best position.

7. In this room the bed is best in Julia's best position, north. A mirror should not reflect the bed, so a small mirror has been used here (see 1).

8. Two square tables, signifying containment, are placed on either side of the bed.

9. A picture of a couple is placed here to symbolize togetherness in the symbolic Relationships area.

10. In the compass Relationships area, which is Earth, stones have been placed on the bathroom and toilet windowsills.

11. A plant is placed on the windowsill here to support William's personal Fire element.

▼ *A floor plan of William and Julia's room after the changes were made. The numbers correspond with the captions in the box, left.*

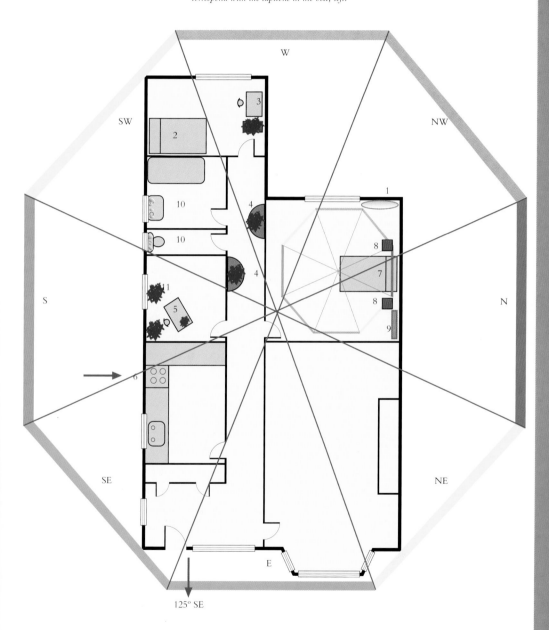

W

SW

NW

S

N

SE

NE

E

125° SE

PUTTING THE PRINCIPLES INTO PRACTICE

Now that we are familiar with the basic principles of Feng Shui, it is time to look at our homes room by room and see if we can arrange them differently to create spaces that will nourish us. When we move energy about there may be unexpected consequences, so it is important to proceed slowly and discover what will work for us. Allow children to create spaces that are meaningful for them at each stage of their development.

HALLS, LOBBIES AND STAIRCASES

When we step though the front door, the first impression we have of a house is the hall. If it is light and spacious with a pleasant, fresh smell, and is clean and tidy, then our spirits will rise. A long dark corridor, the smell of last night's cooking and a stack of newspapers in the corner will set the tone for the whole house. If the energy channels of the house are restricted or blocked, this can have a knock-on effect. Those who live with narrow, dark hallways may suffer restriction mentally or as a blockage in one of their body channels. Psychologically such a place is depressing. It is possible to deal with this by using bright colours and mirrors. Coat hooks at levels to accommodate even the smallest family members and shoe cupboards or racks can all make our

homecoming easier. The last thing we need to see on returning is a mess; we will not look forward to returning home.

THE VIEW FROM THE DOOR

If a door opens immediately on to a wall, people will feel overwhelmed and they will feel life is a struggle. A landscape picture which attracts the eye will give the illusion of drawing us on into the main part of the home. An entrance opposite

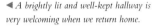
◄ *A brightly lit and well-kept hallway is very welcoming when we return home.*

▼ *Plenty of coat hooks and storage space prevent the hall from becoming cluttered.*

the back door or window will funnel chi straight out and it will not have the opportunity to circulate. Keep doors closed, place plants on windowsills or install coloured glass into the back door window to reflect chi back into the room. If the first room seen from the door is the kitchen, it will be the first port of call on returning home. Food will be on our minds before we do anything else. Children will tumble in on returning from school with outdoor clothes and school bags to raid the fridge. An office opposite the door will encourage us to rush in to check the answerphone. Work will be on our minds and we will not be able to relax. Toilet doors should be kept closed at all times, according to Chinese wisdom, so that we do not watch our wealth being flushed away, and a closed lid is an extra precaution.

▼ *In this spacious hall, natural finishes, and a variety of shapes, colours and textures create an energetic space.*

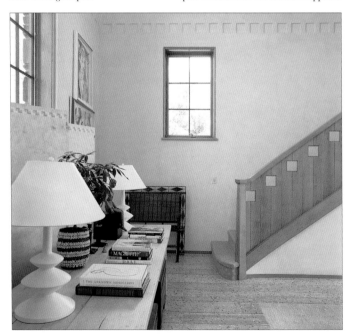

HALL CLUTTER
Coats, Shoes, Bags, Junk mail,
Free papers, Laundry, Items to
take upstairs

COMMUNAL LOBBIES

In buildings which were once large houses but are now small flats, or in badly managed apartment blocks, the communal entrance lobby is often a problem. There are two ways of approaching a dirty, messy, badly decorated lobby: negatively, by blaming others, or by taking positive action. Stuck personal chi is often a contributory factor to stuck energy in a house so it is in the interests of all the occupants to move it.

▼ *Plants either side of the entrance welcome the residents of this apartment block.*

CASE STUDY

Nancy lived in a house that had been converted into four flats, with a communal hallway and staircase. The turnover of residents was high and the communal areas were a mess. Approaches to the landlord and other tenants failed, so Nancy painted the hall herself and put up a shelf with a box for each flat into which she sorted the mail and free papers. A bright poster and a plant completed the project. Almost immediately, the neighbours became more friendly and began to stop for a chat. The turnover of tenants slowed down and within two years Nancy and her neighbours bought the freehold of the property and set about renovating it. As a result the house was transformed and has become a very desirable place to live.

▲ *The front door of this house opens directly on to the stairs. There is no barrier against the chi, which enters through the door and rushes through the house too quickly.*

STAIRCASES

Often the front door of a house or apartment opens straight on to the staircase. Again the chi will be funnelled without having the chance to circulate so it is a good idea to block the view of the stairs by using a plant, a bookcase or other piece of furniture. If this is not possible, a round rug or a crystal chandelier will gather the chi in the hall. A wind chime which sounds as the door opens will also help to slow down the chi.

Some attention should be paid to how staircases and hallways are lit and decorated. Low ceilings can feel restricting and make the moving of furniture difficult, and a steep stairwell causes problems when decorating, but overcoming these difficulties and making the best of your hall and staircase will pay off.

The staircase should be in proportion to the dimensions of the rest of the house. Steep stairs conduct chi too quickly. Modern conversions often have spiral staircases leading to the bedroom area. These are considered inauspicious in Feng Shui because they resemble a corkscrew through the home. Wrap some ivy or green silk around the staircase and make sure a light shines from top to bottom. Stairs with open treads allow the chi to escape. Place plants, real or symbolic, representing Wood energy underneath.

▲ *A large plant placed in this position makes all the difference. It masks the corner of the stairs from view of the front door and slows down the chi.*

CHI FLOW IMPROVEMENT IN A HALLWAY

BEFORE   AFTER

1. Muslin curtains create a pause between the outside and the house.
2. Children and guests leave coats, shoes and umbrellas neatly on hooks and racks. These also block the view of the stairs from the door and hide outer garments from the inside.
3. At the foot of the stairs a mirror reflects a plaster plate with a painted landscape, which has the effect of drawing visitors deeper into the house.
4. The children can go up to their rooms at this point and may not even enter the kitchen until suppertime. If the chi flow upstairs works, they may even have washed their hands first!

LIVING ROOMS

A living room is used for a number of activities – for relaxation, as a family room where games are played, and an entertainment room for watching television and playing music. In some homes, particularly in apartments, the living room may have a dining area attached, or part of it may be used as a study or office space. The arrangement of the room is therefore important if these diverse functions are to be supported successfully.

▼ *Natural materials, lots of colour and a pleasant view give this living room an energetic feeling.*

Living areas should be welcoming, and the colour scheme can help this. Proportion is also important. In barn or warehouse conversions with large open-plan spaces and high ceilings, it is preferable to create small groupings of furniture rather than attempt to create a single room within the space. In small rooms, try to keep bookcases and built-in wall units low, otherwise the room will feel top-heavy and appear to close in. It is especially important to be able to screen off study or office areas so that work is not constantly preying on the mind when we are trying to relax.

SEATING

Living rooms are yin spaces full of comfortable, fabric-covered seats which are also yin. Chairs and sofas with high backs and arms are protective and represent the Tortoise, Dragon, Tiger formation offering support to those who sit in them. A footstool nearby marks the Phoenix position.

Those sitting in the room should, where possible, not sit with their backs to the door. Guests should feel welcome when they come, so offer them the prime positions facing the door. In rooms where chairs and sofas are not backed by

▶ *All these chairs are supportive to the occupants, adding to the peaceful energy of this elegant room.*

a wall, create stability behind the seating by placing a table or bookcase there. Furniture is always best if it has rounded edges. If the bedroom leads off the main living area, make sure that the furniture is not sending a "poison arrow" into the room from a corner. Keep doors from the living room closed.

BACKS TO THE DOOR

If you have a visitor who does more than their fair share of the talking, position them with their back to the door to reduce their dominance in the group. In addition, uninvited guests who you would like to leave as soon as possible should be also be placed outside the main group.

▲ *The Earth colour on the walls and lamps is welcoming, but the blue Water energy drains it.*

▼ *Plenty of Earth colours on the walls and in the furnishing fabrics make this a nurturing and cosy room.*

SEATING ARRANGEMENTS

▲ This seating arrangement is suitable for a harmonious family or social gathering. The "circle" is used in all cultures for community gatherings.

▶ In this arrangement the table is sending a "poison arrow" into the bedroom. Re-position the furniture to prevent this.

▼ The television arrangement spells death to social chat and family unity.

▲ This arrangement is useful for a meeting as it focuses people on whatever is taking place, but also has space to allow the energy in.

FIREPLACES

In previous centuries fires were used for cooking, warmth and protection, and were carefully tended. The communal fire was the focal point of family life. These days a real fire is less common, and when it is present it is often a secondary heat source, lit only at festival times or at weekends, rather than a vital source of life. A coal or wood fire, however, always makes a room feel welcoming and draws family and friends toward it.

Since a fireplace is an opening into the room, a mirror above it is beneficial to symbolically prevent the chi from escaping. A fireguard will be necessary, especially where there are children. Plants positioned on either side of the fireplace represent Wood energy, which will symbolically feed the fire and enhance its gathering qualities.

The chimney wall often juts into the living room, creating alcoves on either side. Be aware of this when placing chairs as people sitting in them may be the recipients of harmful chi from the corners. Soften any jutting angles on the mantelpiece with hanging plants.

LIGHTING

A variety of lighting is necessary, particularly if the room is used for a number of purposes. Bright lighting is required for family activities and for children playing, and also in north-facing rooms which get

▲ *A cosy living area has been created in the middle of this vast space.*

little natural light. In addition, there should be softer lights; uplighters in the corners or wall lights, and task lighting if there is a desk in the room.

SCREENS

Ideally, kitchens and dining rooms should be separate from the main living room. Where they are attached or adjoining, screen them off in some way or food will become too important and grazing habits will be encouraged.

▼ *A larger sofa would give more support in this well-proportioned room.*

A BALANCE OF LIGHT

▲ Here the blue (Water) energy is overpowering the green (Wood) energy and the red (Fire) energy.

▲ The red lamp makes an enormous difference, restoring the balance of the various energies in the room.

TELEVISIONS AND STEREOS

Always arrange the seating so that it does not allow the television to be the main focus of the room. Where the TV is the focal point, instead of a warm, gathering fire, the family will sit in rows and communication will be negligible. (However, this is better than each child having a television in their bedroom, which can

▲ *The additional colours and the mixture of whites turn this into a warm room.*

result in a total breakdown of the social aspects of family life.) Position stereos as far away from seating as possible to avoid electromagnetic radiation.

FURNISHINGS

If the living room is painted in a single colour, small areas of stimulation are necessary to keep the energy moving. Too much fabric can harbour dust and fade, creating stagnant energy, but in a room where people gather curtains help to create a cosy feeling. Undressed windows

◄ *A small television set is far better than a large set that will dominate the room.*

▶ *Natural materials and fresh colour give this room a good feel.*

and ones with blinds can be harsh and, being rectangular, add to the Earth energy of the room. In rooms that have many rectangular features and are also decorated in Earth colours – magnolia, brown, mustard – the energy will feel sluggish and can make the occupants feel depressed. Keep family rooms well-ventilated and allow in as much natural light as possible.

PAINTINGS AND OBJECTS

We should always be aware of the effect of the images with which we surround ourselves, since they reflect our inner selves. Gruesome images and spiky objects can reflect inner turmoil, whereas bells, rainbows and pictures of the seasons will reflect inner peace. If we live alone our living rooms will reflect our desire for a peaceful haven or our need for companionship and we can use the space to create positive atmospheres.

Images and artwork displayed in family spaces should be cheerful and reflect pleasant and harmonious themes. Ideally, photographs of the family should be displayed in this room. If one child is more artistically talented than the others, in the interests of family harmony, his/her achievements should not be spread all round the room or the other children will feel that they are failures by comparison. Guns, swords and other weapons have no place in the living room.

It is important that the contents of the home, especially the communal areas, should be balanced and reflect the lives of all the occupants. If our working lives are hectic, our living rooms will reflect our desire for a peaceful haven. Lonely people should, however, use this room to reflect their need for companionship and remove all single images – such as pictures of lone figures; ornaments should

▲ *This is a room designed for sitting and chatting. The round table ensures the conversation will not get too serious.*

▼ *We should surround ourselves with positive images. The clean lines of this carved wooden bird make the energy soar.*

▼ *This oval urn prevents stagnation in an otherwise gloomy corner.*

be grouped in pairs, and the room should be used to create a positive energy.

Where we share our homes with friends, with a partner, or as part of a family, we need to create personal spaces within which we feel comfortable and where we can express ourselves. Relationships with those whose horoscopes or numbers conflict with our own are common and we will be familiar with the phrase "opposites attract". Formulae may suggest, however, that one partner should live in an east group house and the other a west group house. We have to be practical. Where the energies of a house favour one occupant more than the other, it is important to take this into account and enable the other to express themselves within the house and to position themselves in favourable directions in bed and when working and relaxing.

▶ *We should position ourselves in favourable directions surrounded by supportive images.*

CASE STUDY

When David and Sarah retired to the coast from their family house in the country, they left behind a large garden which Sarah had lovingly tended for 20 years. David, a keen angler, purchased a share in a boat and joined the local fishing club, and soon had a full and active social life. Photographs of his activities, pictures of boats and his prize catch preserved in a glass case along with accompanying trophies appeared around the house. Having decorated the house and finished arranging the tiny garden, Sarah became bored and felt unfulfilled in her new life, but since David was so happy she kept to herself the fact that she preferred life in the country.

As David had an office and a workshop, it was agreed that Sarah should have part of the house designated as her own space and the living room was chosen as her personal area.

1. Sarah, a Water Rooster, was being overwhelmed by too much water in her

new environment. A large plant in the North symbolically drained some of the Water energy.

2. Born in 1934, Sarah's magic number is 3, making her best direction south, so the seating was arranged accordingly.

3. David's fishing trophies and photographs were placed in his study and, since she did not want to hurt his feelings but did not like having dead animals in the house, Sarah compromised and suggested that the prize fish could go into the bathroom and not be banished to the workshop. Sarah framed some watercolours she had painted at their former home and hung them on the wall instead.

4. To dispel the idea that this lifestyle was to be Sarah's lot for the rest of her retirement, and particularly since the windows faced west and the setting sun, the rising growth energy of the east was stimulated with a picture of the rising sun.

5. A mirror placed in the south-east, also representing Wood, reflected the garden

and drew it into the house to support Sarah's love of the countryside.

6. After reading a Feng Shui book, Sarah decided to try to activate the Relationships area to see if she could find new friends. Using the Symbolic Bagua, she put up a poster of a group of people chatting, which was also reflected in the mirror, thus doubling the effect.

When the changes had been made, a neighbour visited and admired Sarah's watercolours and suggested she should display them at the local garden show. Someone admired and purchased them, and with the money Sarah bought a greenhouse where she now grows exotic plants which she paints portraits of and sells. Interestingly, the picture of the rising sun is, according to the Symbolic Bagua, in Sarah's Offspring or Projects area. She is now an active member of a gardening group, where she has made lots of friends and is busy all the time.

DINING ROOMS

The dining room is a social area where family and friends can meet, talk and enjoy good food together. As snacking and "grazing" typify modern eating habits, the dining room has diminished in importance. For the Chinese it is a centre of wealth, where a full table, often mirrored to apparently double the quantity, is indicative of the financial standing of the family.

Dining room colours should be bright

▶ If there is a window behind the dining table, it is important that the chairs have backs to them for support.

▲ This wonderful dining room has a lovely view of the garden. Small shelves would protect diners from the axe-like glass overhead.

and stimulating to whet the appetite. Dull, lifeless colours should be avoided as they suppress the appetite. Lighting should be chosen with care to complement the food and not cast shadows over the table. Candles can be romantic, but may get in the way when people are serving themselves or become irritating if they are too tall or flicker. Beware of pictures and ornaments that conjure up inappropriate images – hunting scenes or

▲ *A lovely setting for a meal. The candles are low enough not to get in the way or prevent people seeing each other properly.*

▼ *An excellent dining room – the chairs are backed by a wall and the mirror reflects the table, doubling its apparent size.*

▲ *Kitchen diners make a good setting for an informal meal, and round tables are ideal as they encourage lively conversation.*

▶ *Low candles such as these pretty shell candles are safer than tall ones at the table.*

a china pig collection are not suitable if you have vegetarian friends. The best images to display are ones of fruit, the fresh, clean outdoors, or of friends dining. If mirrors are used, position them so that diners will not feel uncomfortable.

High-backed solid chairs, preferably with arms, represent the supportive Tortoise, Tiger, Dragon formation. Sitting positions are considered to be very important. The prime positions in the room should have a solid wall behind them and a view of the door. The most vulnerable positions are those with a door behind them, followed by seats with their backs to a window.

Table shapes are also important and can affect the quality of the meal. Round tables tend to make your guests leave early because the chi spins round them, while square tables allow more stability. Rectangular tables are difficult as those at either end tend to feel left out. The best shaped tables are octagonal, which not only enable guests to interact with everyone else on the table, but also represent the Cosmos as reflected in the Bagua.

BALANCED EATING

Much has been made of balanced eating recently but this is not a new concept. Since ancient times, diet has formed part of the same philosophy as Feng Shui. Meals are planned to create a yin-yang balance and with the nature of the Five Elements in mind. Some foods are regarded as having yin qualities and some yang, and different tastes are associated with the Five Elements.

We should learn to recognize the signals that our bodies and our state of mind give out and recognize whether we are becoming yin (feeling tired and slowing down) or yang (unable to relax and stressed). We can balance our diets by ensuring we eat the same proportion of

▲ *Conservatory dining rooms are becoming popular and can create light, spacious areas for eating in all the year round.*

◄ *In such a large area as this your guests might feel slightly ill-at-ease. High-backed chairs would help dispel any nervousness. A round table is a good shape for this room.*

yin foods – such as alcohol, chocolate, citrus fruits, coffee and sugar – and yang foods – such as cheese, eggs, meat, pulses and salt.

Yin and yang attributes are attached to each of the Five Elements, and in Chinese medicine herbs and other remedies, including food, are recommended in order to maintain a healthy and balanced body. In northern countries (yin) there is a tendency and need to consume more cooked foods (yang) while in southerly areas (yang) more raw foods are consumed. Eating native products in season is highly recommended.

TASTES AND THE ELEMENTS				
Wood	**Fire**	**Earth**	**Metal**	**Water**
spring	summer	late summer	autumn	winter
sour	bitter	sweet	pungent	salt
yin	yang	yin	yin	yang

THE BAGUA AND FAMILY SEATING

We have seen that each sector of the Bagua can represent several things. The sectors are associated with particular manifestations of the energy of one of the Five Elements – in its yin or yang form. Each also represents a certain type of energy reflecting a direction, season or time period. The Symbolic Bagua suggests the journey of life, with each sector representing a particular aspect – career, wealth, relationships and so on.

Here we look at the energies of each sector in terms of the family. In the past the Bagua may have been used to allocate rooms in a house, but great fun can be had using the Bagua in seating plans at the dining table. The diagram (right) shows the arrangement of family members around the Bagua. Each represents the energy of the direction they fall within, and this can add further insight into the qualities of

the energy in that location. Bear in mind that we are looking at centuries-old imagery; house-husbands and executive mothers should appreciate that this is an energetic quality, not stereotyping.

FATHER: Representative of solidity, the leader and the head of the household. Sometimes called the Creative energy.

MOTHER: Complements the Father. A

nurturing, supporting energy. Also known as Receptive energy.

ELDEST SON: Also known as the energy of Thunder and the Dragon, whose energy erupts from below and soars upwards.

ELDEST DAUGHTER: Called the Gentle energy, this energy is perceptive and supportive and represents growth.

MIDDLE SON: Sometimes called the Abysmal energy, which suggests hard work without much reward.

MIDDLE DAUGHTER: A Clinging energy, representing a fire, bright and impenetrable outside but burning-out and weakness within.

YOUNGEST SON: Also called the Mountain energy, suggesting a firm stillness and waiting.

YOUNGEST DAUGHTER: Also known as the Joyful, or the Lake, which suggests a deep inward energy or stubbornness and a weak, excitable exterior.

THE DINNER PARTY

The Bagua can be used for all sorts of social occasions. Imagine that an executive is retiring from your company and you and a rival are in the running for the job. You arrange a dinner party and invite your boss, your rival and a young employee who reminds you of yourself when younger and whom you have taken under your wing. You can use the Bagua to seat your colleagues

and their partners to ensure that you will get the job.

Out of respect, the boss and his/her partner are in the prime positions. When the boss is not giving any attention to the vivacious spouse of your protégé (with his back thus turned to your rival) and is concentrating on eating, the first people he/she will see when he/she looks up are you and your partner, and also your protégé. Your rival, seated in the worst position, representing hard toil for no reward, and his partner are too far apart to be able to support each other. The attention of the boss's spouse is taken up by

the bubbly person chatting to the boss, and your partner opposite. After several attempts at conversation, with no support, your rival's spouse gives up. The result is that you get the job, and your protégé moves into your shoes.

◀ *Manipulate situations by using ancient interpretations of the energies of the Bagua.*

▶ *Whatever the occasion or intention a decorated table with well-presented, nourishing food will be supportive.*

KITCHENS

The kitchen is probably the most important room in the house and, being multi-functional, often the most difficult room to deal with. Apart from its primary purpose for storing, preparing and consuming food, it is a meeting place for family and friends, a children's play area and occasionally even an office. More than any other room, the kitchen holds clues to a person's lifestyle. It is the health centre of our lives and it is important that it functions well and supports us.

The direction a kitchen faces has a powerful effect on its function. In ancient China, kitchens were open to the southeast to catch the breezes that would help ignite the cooking stove. This practical application of Feng Shui reflects the principle of living in harmony with nature. When we have discovered in which direction our kitchen lies, we can use "The Relationships of the Five Elements" table to help us create balance.

A red kitchen facing south will be overloaded with yang Fire energy which needs to be drained. "The Relationships of the Five Elements" table shows that Earth drains Fire, so incorporating a stone floor or some stone pots would be appropriate. As the Fire element is far too dominant, representation of the Water element in the form of a picture of water or a blue blind or tablecloth would also considerably lessen the effect. Plants would not be advisable here since they belong to the Wood element,

▲ *Left: Chi rushes through this kitchen, creating a feeling of discomfort.*
Right: Ceiling lights and plants by the window slow down the chi and contain it.

which feeds Fire and makes it stronger. In the case of all kitchens, the Fire element, represented by the cooker and electrical cooking appliances, is in conflict with Water, represented by actual water and the fridge. A delicate balance has to be maintained.

Some modern kitchens are so streamlined that nothing is on display. Since the major features consist of only one or two colours or materials, the kitchen can appear lifeless. Sometimes a dash of red, or a green plant can bring a room to life. Ideally, kitchens should contain something from each of the elements.

THE STOVE

The stove is considered to be of great importance. Where possible, the energy source which flows into it, the electric

▲ *Task lighting is ideal in kitchens. Here it gives focus in a high-ceilinged room, where other lights would cast shadows.*

socket or the gas pipe, should be in your most auspicious location. It is important not to feel vulnerable while standing at the stove. The reasoning behind this is that, since food is the prime source of nourishment and health for the family, it is important that the cook should not feel jumpy or the food will be spoiled through lack of concentration.

A reflective surface positioned behind the cooker, or a chrome cake tin or toaster nearby, will enable the cook to be aware of anyone entering the room. A wind chime or other sound device activated by the door opening will also serve the same purpose.

▲ *The kitchen stove is the heart of the home and should face in an auspicious direction.*

▲ *If you cook with your back to the door, shiny objects can reflect the space behind you.*

▲ *Keep your cooking area as clutter-free as possible.*

CHI FLOW IN THE KITCHEN

As elsewhere in the house, chi should be able to circulate freely round the kitchen. It cannot do this if the kitchen door is in direct line with the outside doors and windows since it is channelled straight through. If this is the case, you should aim to slow it down by physical or psychological barriers. The simplest method is to keep the door closed. Barriers could include furniture, vegetable trolleys or large plants. More subtle methods such as mobiles, lampshades and colour can be used to create visual and psychological barriers. Barriers can be detrimental, however, and a tall fridge or cupboard by the door will block the natural flow of chi into the room.

Fast-moving chi is not the only problem. Stagnant chi is particularly harmful in a kitchen. It can occur in a room with

▲ *Smooth, rounded lines allow the chi to move gently around this lovely kitchen.*

◀ *In a kitchen where the chi flows straight out of the window, place some red glass, plants or another barrier on the windowsill to slow it down.*

▼ *Eye-level cupboards over the cooking area are oppressive; open shelves would be better.*

CASE STUDY

This typical modern kitchen has both good and bad points.

1 The cooker, sink and fridge are in an excellent triangle formation.

2 The corner of this work surface has been rounded off so there are no "poison arrows" which otherwise would have pointed at the chairs.

3 The energy is not moving in this corner. A plant or mirror here will help to move the chi along.

4 The chairs have their backs to the door and are vulnerable. A large plant or vegetable basket would act as a barrier. Alternatively, the table and chairs could move out of the corner so the door is visible from each chair.

no window and poor circulation, or in a room with dark inaccessible corners. One cause of this is simply having too much furniture in the room, which impedes movement. If we catch our hip on the corner of a table each time we need to

KITCHEN CLUTTER

Rotting fruit and vegetables
Out-of-date packets and jars
Unlabelled boxes in the freezer
Unused gadgets
Rarely used electrical appliances
Over-full waste bins
Odd pieces of crockery
Plastic bags
Bits of string
Laundry
Crumbs
Fallen plant leaves
Things which "might come in handy"

get to the fridge our body chi will not flow as it should because we are forever twisting to avoid it. At the end of a long day, a ready-made meal may seem an easier option than dodging the furniture to obtain fresh ingredients from the fridge. Rather than put things away, we may be

tempted to leave out milk bottles and food, which can have health risks as well as cluttering up the kitchen.

Piles of newspapers, overflowing rubbish bins, crumbs and stains on work surfaces all represent stagnant chi. Another undesirable feature of many apartment kitchens is the cat-litter tray. Bathrooms and toilets are not desirable near a kitchen because of the antipathy of the Water element to the Fire element of the kitchen, as well as for more obvious reasons. If we take trouble with the location of our own toilets and bathrooms, we should also give serious thought to those of our pets.

Pointed corners are a feature of most kitchens – the edges of appliances, the corners of work surfaces, knives, shelf edges and the edges of slatted blinds all send out chi that makes us feel uncomfortable. Knives should be kept out of sight in a drawer and work surfaces should have rounded edges, if possible. Among the worst sources of this inauspicious chi, known as "poison arrows", are wall cupboards. Most of us have banged our heads on an open door, but even when shut the cupboards can be oppressive. There is a tendency to store far too

much in the kitchen – out-of-date jars, gadgets we never use, a dinner service we only bring out on special occasions or when the person who gave it to us visits. If we examine the contents of the kitchen, we will probably be able to throw away or relocate many items to give us more space and enable the chi to flow. There are many useful storage systems available which will enable us to make optimum use of the space.

▼ *Efficient storage systems reduce kitchen clutter; review the contents regularly.*

▲ *Waist-high cupboards by a work surface are preferable to overhead ones, which can be oppressive, especially in a small kitchen. Keep any frequently used equipment to hand and store cooking equipment, rather than crockery or food, inside cupboards that are adjacent to an oven.*

THE HEALTHY KITCHEN

Kitchens appeal to all our senses. Magazine pictures tantalizingly portray them as rooms featuring bowls of fresh fruit and views over lawns and flower beds. Healthy, freshly prepared meals can be seen on tables where friends and family gather to socialize. Delicious smells, tastes, merry sounds, abundance and happiness radiate from these pages but the reality is often different. Modern kitchens, far from supporting and stimulating us, can unbalance and affect us negatively. The noise from kitchen gadgets, the contamination of food by substances used in packaging, dangers posed by the cleaning agents we use on our work surfaces, the chemicals used in food production, all serve to assault our senses and diminish our well-being.

▲*There is plenty of Wood in this country-style kitchen, which provides excellent levels of energy.*

CASE STUDY

Mary's kitchen was dark and oppressive. The small area in front was a particular problem because the staircase formed a deep slope, and the space on the left was too narrow for conventional units. The main area felt claustrophobic, with work surfaces and wall cupboards sending out chi in the form of "poison arrows". The cooker could not be moved to face Mary's best direction but this was considered secondary to getting the chi flow right.

1. Red, yellow and green opaque glass was used in the south-facing door and window overlooking a brick wall to stimulate the south Fire element. The light coming through the glass sent a rainbow effect into the room which stimulated the chi there.

2. The plants on the windowsill were placed to stimulate the Wood element of the East.

3. The work triangle is in place. Care was taken not to place the fridge opposite the cooker, so there is no conflict between the Fire and Water elements.

4. Pale yellow cupboards and a terracotta container in the north-east introduced the Earth element.

5. Stainless steel pans hung in the north-west stimulate the Metal area.

6. These oddly sized and shaped walls were made into cupboards to make the shape regular. The one on the right was built over and around the washing machine and drier. Glass doors were put in front of the window to enable the coloured light to shine in. Mary placed her china collection on glass shelves here.

BEDROOMS

The bedroom is considered to be one of the most important rooms of the house in Feng Shui. Adults spend a third of their lives in bed, while children and teenagers often spend even more than this. We must therefore be certain that these rooms are suitable for relaxing and regenerating us, as well as for encouraging romance in our lives.

BEDS

A bed should face in one of our auspicious directions, which means that the top of our heads should point that way when we are lying down. Where partners have different auspicious directions, there has to be a compromise; for example, if the house is a West group house and favours one partner, then the bed direction should favour the other.

The best bed position is diagonally opposite the door. The element of surprise is never recommended in the bedroom. If the occupants of the bed do not have a reasonable view of the door, a mirror should be placed to reflect anyone entering. Having the foot of the bed in direct line with the door is known as the "mortuary position" in China because coffins are placed in that position when awaiting collection.

Doors and windows situated opposite each other are not considered auspicious. If a line of chi between two windows – or a door and window – crosses the bed, this is thought to cause illness.

▲ *Four-poster beds can be claustrophobic if they have heavy wood and elaborate fabric canopies, but this elegant bamboo bed without any excess curtaining gives a very light effect.*

▼ *The symmetry of the tables and lamps at each side of this bed is perfect. Each side of the bed should have identical furnishings.*

▼ *Here the view of the garden is auspicious, but less spiky ornaments behind the bed would be better for relaxation.*

▼ *This soft, dreamy room is very restful. Do not have too many books in the bedroom as they are mentally stimulating.*

FURNISHINGS

Images in the bedroom should be in pairs, particularly in the Relationships corner of the room. Images of a solitary figure in a single person's bedroom indicate loneliness, as does a single bed. It is possible to feel isolated and insecure within a marriage. If this is the case, hang a picture of a couple on the wall and display pairs of objects. Photographs of parents, children or friends have no place in a couple's bedroom.

Mirrors in the bedroom should not face the bed. The Chinese believe that the soul leaves the body as we sleep and will be disconcerted to come across itself in the mirror. A modern interpretation

Ideally, beds should be raised off the floor with enough space for air to circulate underneath. Storage drawers full of old clothes and crates of old magazines and other items stored beneath them create a stagnant chi which is not desirable.

Beds should be made of natural materials which can breathe. Wood is the usual choice although bamboo is also used. People belonging to the Metal element often favour metal beds. Since metal conducts heat and electricity, be very careful to keep electrical equipment and heaters away from the bed. Water beds are not recommended because they cause conflict between Fire, the electrical heating source, and Water, as well as creating instability while we sleep.

Headboards offer support but should always be tightly secured. They represent the Tortoise position, and as such, should be higher than the Phoenix, or the footboard. Beds should be backed by a wall, not a window, which feels insecure and can let in draughts.

Where a double bed is in a confined space and one occupant has to climb over the other to get in or out, harmony will not prevail. The best position for a bed is with a wall behind and enough room on either side for a small table or cupboard. These should always be balanced at either side; one will not do.

▲ *Headboards offer support and this magnificent carved wooden headboard is a particularly fine example.*

▼ *This is an attractive bedroom but the mirror should not reflect the bed. En suite bathrooms are not recommended either.*

CASE STUDY

Although Joe and Amy had a comfortable house, lovely children and were blessed in all aspects of their lives, they revealed separately that they felt lonely and isolated. A look at the bedroom revealed all. On a shelf opposite the bed sat a TV, video and stereo system. Joe enjoyed watching videos in bed and waking up to his favourite rock bands. Amy disliked Joe's choice of videos and her collection of self-improvement books on relationships and stress sat on the next shelf. On the top shelf were photographs of the children, and a box of toys to keep them amused when they came in early in the morning was on the bottom shelf. On the walls to either side of Joe and Amy's bed an image of a solitary man and woman gazed wistfully at each other across the room.

Following the Feng Shui consultation, the toys were removed to the children's rooms, where they were encouraged to play on waking. The two pictures were placed side by side, where the wistful gaze could turn into a lustful glance, and the TV, video and stereo were relocated. Joe is no longer worried that Amy is miserable and unfulfilled as she no longer has need of her books.

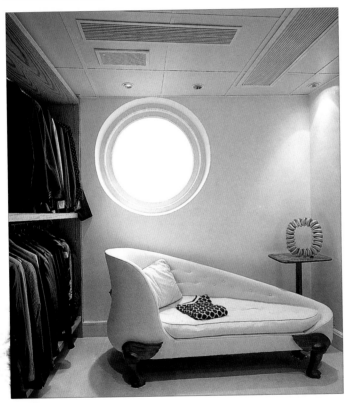

▲ *A dressing room is ideal as it frees the bedroom for rest and romance.*

might be that most of us are not at our best in the mornings and would not want our tousled image to be the first thing we see on waking. It would be much better to see a picture of the sun rising or a fresh green landscape. Street lights outside the room can also create reflective images in a mirror, which may disturb us when we are half-asleep. In contrast, strategically placed mirrors facing a wonderful view will draw it into the room.

The bedroom should not become a storage area or an office, nor serve any function other than romance and sleep. If you have space in your house, dressing rooms are ideal since they remove most extraneous things from the bedroom. Most bedrooms, however, contain wardrobes and drawer space. Keeping these clear of clutter means we can close them easily and make sure we have plenty of room to hang up our clothes. Garments strewn over chairs for days on end constitute clutter and worry us psychologically since we know we will have to deal with them eventually. The worst form of storage is the overhead cupboard linking wardrobes on either side of the bed. This acts in the same way as a beam and can leave those sleeping under it feeling vulnerable. The same applies to anything else hanging over the bed.

ELECTRICAL EQUIPMENT

Electrical equipment in the bedroom is not desirable for two reasons. First, it detracts from the main functions of the

▼ *The beam over this double bed symbolically divides the couple occupying the bed.*

more time to eat a proper breakfast in the morning and are more punctual for work when they have to get out of bed to turn off the alarm.

It is surprising how many people have telephones sitting on bed-side tables. They have no place in a bedroom as they prevent relaxation, especially if late night social calls are common. The best place for mobile phones outside office hours is in a briefcase, switched off; everyone is entitled to some time for themselves.

▶ *A harp has been placed in the Wealth corner of this room to lift the energy of the sloping wall.*

room. Secondly, the harmful electromagnetic waves that are generated can have an adverse effect on those sleeping there. Ionizers positioned close to a bed present the most serious threat, but even clock radios send out waves over a considerable distance.

Electric blankets are a real problem because they encase the bed in an electromagnetic field. They should be unplugged from the wall before anyone gets into bed.

All electrical items should be on the opposite side of the room from the bed, and this includes electrical clocks. One advantage of this is that it makes the snooze button redundant. People find

▼ *Cramped spaces under slanting walls are not recommended in Feng Shui as they restrict the flow of chi.*

BED POSITIONS

1. If the bed is positioned so that the occupant cannot see who is entering, place a mirror opposite the door.

2. When the foot of the bed is in direct line with the door, this is known in China as the "mortuary position".

3. A line of harmful chi crosses this bed from two facing windows.

4. A mirror opposite a window can draw in wonderful views.

THE NURSERY

Medical research has shown that pollutants in decorating materials and furniture may be responsible for breathing difficulties and cot deaths in susceptible babies. Decorate the room for a new baby as long as possible before it is due and air the room thoroughly. If this cannot be done, put the baby in the parents' room until the smell of fresh paint has disappeared. Decorating materials should be manufactured from natural products and cot bedding preferably made from natural untreated fibres.

STIMULATING THE SENSES

We can help small children to distinguish colours and shapes by providing them with suitable stimulation. A mobile hung above the foot of a baby's cot will keep it fascinated for a long time and provide comfort before it falls asleep. Do not place one directly over the head of the baby as this can be threatening.

Very small children could be suffocated if furry toy animals fall on their faces so keep these out of the cot but place

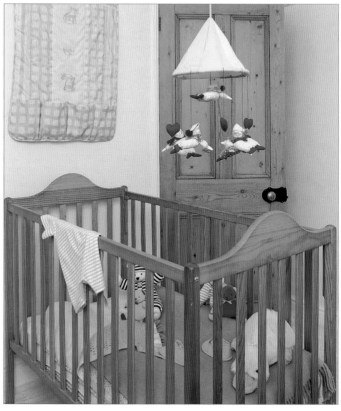

▶ *This is a bright, cheerful room with plenty of stimulation for a baby.*

▼ *Bright colours and shapes give lots of visual appeal during the day.*

▼ *A chalkboard gives a child scope for freedom of expression.*

▼ *This large chest will take many toys and keep the room free from clutter.*

▲ *This first bed for a young child has a canopy to keep it cosy.*

them where the baby can see them, perhaps on a nearby shelf. A bright wall frieze can also occupy a baby's attention, as can a large colourful poster.

Sound can be introduced in a number of ways. Fractious babies who do not sleep well may be soothed by taped music, and the sound of voices from a radio may help the insecure to fall asleep. Musical mobiles can be useful in lulling a baby to sleep, but they might be disturbed if you have to keep rewinding the mobile. Babies soon learn to do things themselves and the look of wonder on its face as a child discovers it can make something happen is magical. By tying bells and rattles to the bars of the cot we help the child on its way to independence, but these are best not left in the cot at night or they will disturb its sleep.

The sense of touch is stimulated by numerous textures – furry, soft, hard and smooth. Allow your child access to a variety of experiences but secure playthings to the cot or you will be forever picking them up from the floor. Do not be tempted to introduce manufactured smells to small children as they are too strong. The familiar smell of a mother or well-loved teddy is far better. At teething time, ensure that all materials which can be put into the mouth conform to safety standards and that cot paint is lead-free.

POSSIBLE HAZARDS

Pets can be a problem if they snuggle up to the baby for warmth or become jealous of the attention it receives. Suitable

safety precautions should be taken inside the home. As children begin to crawl, and later to walk and climb, ensure that all fires and electrical sockets are securely covered, that windows are secure and stairs have barriers at the top and bottom.

▲ *Brightly decorated furnishings in this bedroom lift the energy in a dark corner.*

▼ *Wood energy, symbolized by the frieze of trees, suits the growing child, who needs to be allowed freedom of expression.*

CHILDREN'S ROOMS

Children's rooms can be a challenge as they often need to fulfil two opposing functions – sleep and play. Although parents aim to ensure that sleep takes place at night and play during the day, a look at some children's rooms indicates why they do not always get it the right way round as there is no division between the two. Children's rooms should also support them and their needs as they grow. Where a room is shared, each child should have a private space within it that they feel is their own.

The energy of the east with the rising sun in the morning is ideal for children. The west with the setting sun at night is good for hyperactive children who cannot settle, although this direction is normal-

▼ Plenty of storage space means that toys can be neatly stacked away.

ly better for elderly people to sleep in.

The heads of beds should face their supportive directions, although this is not always possible when there is more than one child in the room. It is more important that they should feel safe, and a view of the door is essential for children. Rooms with dark corners which house strange shapes and cast shadows on the walls can prove disturbing for young children with vivid imaginations.

BEDS

Wooden beds are preferable because they do not pick up electromagnetic radiation. Bunk beds are not considered suitable since they depress the chi, both of the child on top who is close to the ceiling and the one underneath who has a body above, often a fidgety one. Canopies over the bed have the same effect and can also

▲ *A stark, but restful child's room. The bed would be better backed by the wall.*

harbour dust. Cupboards and beams can also have a debilitating effect. Children's beds should have a headboard and should not back on to a window or a door.

DECORATION

As children grow, mentally as well as physically, part of the learning process is to be able to make choices. Children instinctively know the type of energy

CLUTTER IN CHILDREN'S ROOMS
Broken, irreparable toys
Outgrown toys
Books they never look at
Outgrown clothes
Dry felt-tip pens
Games and jigsaw puzzles with pieces missing

▲ *A reassuring first bed for a young child, as the canopy offers protection.*

their rooms as this must inevitably isolate them from their families and hamper their social interaction outside. Apart from this consideration, the electromagnetic radiation from TVs and computers in children's bedrooms is a cause for concern, particularly as these rooms are often small and confine the electro-pollution. Where possible, remove all electrical items from children's rooms and relocate them in other areas of the house.

▼ *Low windows can create a fear of falling, the puppet theatre here acts as a screen.*

they require to support them and should be allowed to design their own bedrooms and have a major say in the decoration and colours, even if it is not to the parents' taste. We can always shut the door and we should respect it when it is shut. Children need their privacy as we do and if we set an example by knocking and asking permission to enter, then we can expect the same in return.

If there is a family room or playroom elsewhere, then excessive stimulation in the form of toys should not be a problem in the bedroom. Where the room serves a dual purpose, create a separate sleeping area and provide storage for toys to be put away out of sight at night.

FURNISHINGS

If the floor is hard, a soft rug by the bed is welcoming in the morning and will give a gentle start to the day. Furniture with curved corners helps to prevent minor accidents. If your child has chosen

the colours, you can select shades and hues to suit the child's personality – cooler ones to balance an active child and brighter ones to stimulate a more reticent personality.

It is disturbing how many very small children have their own television sets in

▼ *A child's room should give her or him the space and facility to read and be creative.*

TEENAGERS' ROOMS

▲ *The high, sloping ceilings do not impinge on this modern room.*

Teenagers' rooms are evolving places where children who are growing into adults can express themselves – their happiness, their loves, their hurts and their anger. The latter may be directed against us if we attempt to curb their individuality and try to impose our personalities and values on the private space that will nurture them through to adulthood. The needs and the tastes of a thirteen-year-old are very different from those of a seventeen- or eighteen-year-old, and the room may be changed on almost an annual basis. Some principles will remain constant, however. We can encourage our child to place their beds in an auspicious position and introduce

▼ *This is a pretty room for a young teenage girl beginning to move away from childhood.*

them to Feng Shui, which they may come to regard as a help when they encounter some of the usual trials of growing up.

Older teenagers' rooms are multi-functional and usually act as bedroom, study, sitting room and entertainment area for their friends. It is no wonder that their occupants sometimes become

> ### TEENAGE CLUTTER
> Sweet wrappings and crisp packets
> Unwashed clothes
> Over-flowing wastebins
> Do not touch anything else
> in a teenager's private space

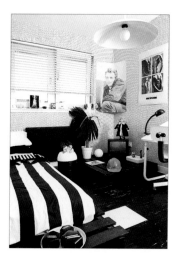

▲ *Black and white – a bold colour choice – is popular with teenagers.*

confused. Teenagers need our support when they ask for it, even though they do not welcome unsolicited advice. They require their own space, physically and intellectually, but they also need positive affirmation from adults. Hold out against a television in the bedroom and encourage the use of family rooms. A computer in the study will draw teenagers out of their bedrooms and preserve this space for sleep and relaxation.

▼ *The bright decor and pretty feel of this room might not suit an older teenager.*

CASE STUDY

Marie, aged sixteen, was going through an "awkward" phase. Her mother, Ella, was at her wits' end trying to get her out of bed in the mornings to catch the one bus guaranteed to get her to school on time. Every morning was a battle, and the resentment festered throughout the day and affected family harmony in the evening. Homework was left undone and Marie's studies were suffering.

A Metal Ox, Marie could be stubborn and, although a girl of few words, she occasionally exploded. Her arrogant manner irritated her father, a Fire Ox, who didn't take kindly to being opposed or to Marie's surliness. He became impatient with his wife, an Earth Goat, who knew Marie needed support and was torn between them in arguments.

Ella decided to take action and offered to redecorate Marie's bedroom and let her choose the decor. Out to shock, Marie chose purple for her room and was surprised when her mother, who knew purple to be stimulating for the mind and good for raising self-esteem, acquiesced.

1. Ella took Marie to a fashionable store and invited her to choose something for her room. As she had hoped, Marie chose a multi-coloured bead curtain for the window.

2. Ella suggested that Marie should turn her bed around so that she could see the curtain.

3. Ella removed the old square bedside table, since the square shape symbolizes containment, and ordered a round one.

4. The alarm clock was placed on Marie's desk so she no longer had access to the snooze button and had to get up to turn it off.

5. To go on the new round table Ella gave Marie a framed photograph showing the family boarding a plane to go on holiday; this energized the "Family" area of the Bagua.

6. Taking a chance, Ella purchased two huge silk sunflowers and suggested they would look lovely in the top right-hand corner of the room – the Earth "Relationships" area of the Bagua represented by the magic number 2.

Now when Ella calls Marie in the morning, she opens the window slightly so the bead curtain moves and tinkles, stimulating the chi. When the alarm rings later Marie has to get out of bed to turn it off, but she is already awake. Family harmony has been restored and they meet on friendly terms more often. Feng Shui is a mixture of common sense and psychology as well as harnessing unseen forces of the universe.

BATHROOMS

The position of the bathroom is considered to be important in Feng Shui because water is synonymous with wealth, and thus the disposal of waste water symbolizes the dispersal of the family fortune. Changing climatic conditions have highlighted how precious a commodity water is, and that measures should be taken not to waste it. Conservationists recommend saving water from baths and sinks to water gardens. Dripping taps are symbolic of wealth running away. When we consider that a dripping tap, leaking at a rate of one drip per second, wastes 1,000 litres (264 gallons) per year, we can see the sense in applying ancient rules to modern problems. Baths and sinks which are clogged, apart from being a constant

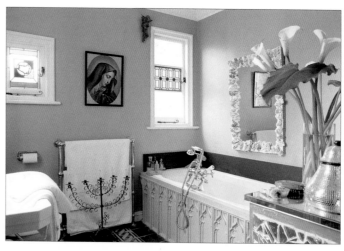

▲ *This spacious and opulent bathroom provides room to relax in.*

source of irritation, can also be a health risk so it is important that we fix them as soon as possible.

▼ *No need for morning queues in this large and airy bathroom.*

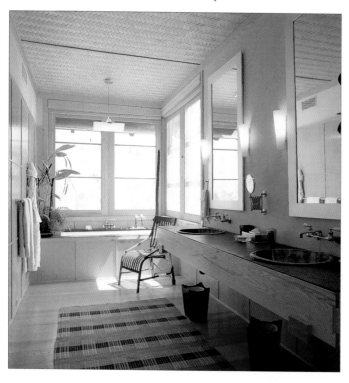

POSITION

Bathrooms should be positioned well away from the front door as this is not an image we want visitors to our homes to subconsciously take away. It is most important not to have bathrooms close to kitchens for health reasons, but they should also be away from dining and sitting areas so that guests won't be embarrassed to use them.

TOILETS

It is not desirable to see the toilet on entering the bathroom and, if possible, it should be situated where it is hidden from view. Screens can be utilized or the toilet positioned behind the door. Toilet doors should be closed and the seat cover closed at all times.

Bathrooms are considered to be linked to the body's plumbing system so a large bathroom using too much water can lead to health problems concerned with evacuation, while cramped bathrooms are connected with restriction in bodily functions. Large bathrooms are also associated with vanity and an excessive obsession with cleanliness, whereas small bathrooms are restricting and can cause accidents as people manoeuvre round.

MIRRORS AND CABINETS

The use of mirrors can give the illusion of more space. Generally, mirrors opposite each other are not considered to be auspicious in Feng Shui because they conjure up an image of constant movement away from the self, with no grounding influences. However, unless

▼ *Use plants and coloured towels to balance the Water element in a bathroom.*

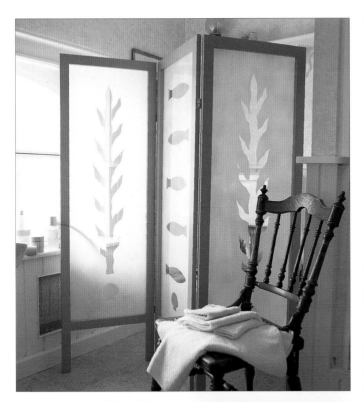

▲ *Screens can be used to hide the bathroom from an entrance or en suite bedroom.*

▶ *The reflective materials in this bathroom help to counteract its heavy ceiling. A large plant or dash of colour would also help.*

▼ *Curvy, watery lines and Metal shapes work well in this unusual bathroom.*

we spend a vast amount of time in front of the bathroom mirror, this is acceptable if it improves the suggestion of space. Mirror tiles are not recommended, or those which in any way cut the image. Fixed mirrors are preferred to those which jut out from walls and normal mirrors are preferred to magnifying mirrors that distort the image.

Bathroom cabinets are places where stagnant chi can easily accumulate. Most cosmetics have a limited shelf life and many cabinets contain items dating back years. There is a limit to the number of eye baths, tweezers and combs which are required in a lifetime.

En Suite Bathrooms

The growing trend to have en suite bathrooms is not in accordance with Feng Shui rules. Where possible, create a separate room for the toilet or else make sure the bathroom area in the bedroom has a well-maintained ventilation system. En suite bathrooms that have been built into the bedroom often create an L-shape with a corner jutting into the room, so action needs to be taken to ensure that this does not point at the bed.

Clutter in the Bathroom

Full waste bins
Empty bottles and toothpaste tubes
Unnecessary soap dishes
Unpolished mirrors
Out-of-date medication
Untried cosmetic samples
Bath oils and perfumes which are never used

▲ *A good balance of colours, elements, plants and natural materials raises the energy in this bathroom.*

▶ *Keep any clutter in the bathroom down to its absolute minimum and keep any soap dishes or holders clean and unclogged.*

Relaxation

Very few of us find the time to relax sufficiently and this often affects our health, both physical and mental. The bathroom is one of the few places where we can escape from the world and be alone. Bathrooms should be decorated so as to enable us to wind down at the end of a busy day, or allow us some peaceful moments in the morning.

ylang are used to alleviate irritability and to create a peaceful mood. The bath is an ideal place for self-massage while taking a bath or having just had one. Try stroking one of these oils towards the heart to stimulate the circulation.

Taoists consider that the nutrition we receive from the air when we breathe is more valuable to us than food and water. As we inhale we draw in energy, which provides energy; when we exhale, we cleanse and detoxify our bodies. The art of breathing properly has been part of the Chinese health regime for centuries, and is based on balancing yin and yang and creating the correct chi flow around the body. It is thought that illness occurs when the correct chi flow is not maintained. Use your time in the bathroom to practise controlled breathing.

Meditation is another relaxation technique. The Chinese call it "sitting still and doing nothing", which is a deceptively simple description of an art that can take years to perfect. Whether our aim is to reflect on the day or to let our minds wander freely and wind down, the bathroom is the ideal place.

▲ *An ideal bathroom – it would be difficult to resist rushing home to relax in this at the end of a hard day.*

▶ *The huge mirror doubles the space in this elegant bathroom. A frame to the top and bottom would contain the chi.*

The colours we use to decorate the bathroom affect how we feel there. Blue is a soothing colour, associated with serenity and contemplation. Colour therapists believe that it lowers the blood pressure, promotes deeper exhalation and induces sleep. Green, on the other hand, rests the eyes and calms the nerves. Whatever colours we choose, we can create a space to relax and soothe ourselves by playing gentle music and by adding a few drops of essential oils to the bathwater. Bergamot, lavender and geranium alleviate stress and anxiety, while camomile, rose, lemon balm and ylang

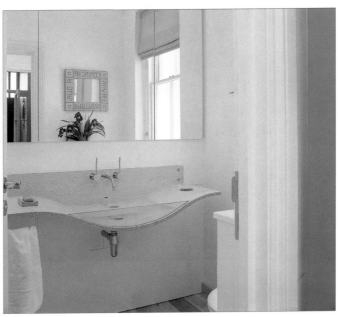

CONSERVATORIES

Conservatories are a popular way of extending our homes and they act as a mediating space between the garden and the house. Ancient Chinese architects designed homes and gardens to interconnect and regarded each as being essential to balance the other. Glimpses through windows and latticed grilles gave views over lakes and vistas, and gardens were planted right up to the house.

Some conservatories are used for plants or as garden rooms, and are places to sit in to relax. Others have become an integral part of the home, taking on the role of dining room, sitting room and in some cases kitchen. Depending on its purpose and aspect, the conservatory can be decorated in various ways.

THE CONSERVATORY KITCHEN

The conservatory kitchen can become very warm in the summer and adequate ventilation will be necessary. It is not considered auspicious to have a glass roof in the kitchen because the symbolic wealth, the food, will evaporate away. Practically speaking, it is not comfortable to work with the sun, or with the rain, beating down above, and a blind or

▼ *This conservatory opens into the kitchen, enabling the cook to join in the conversation.*

▲ *A conservatory is a glorious place to relax in all weathers.*

▶ *An indoor garden which opens into a family kitchen, the conservatory provides an ideal outlook when eating or preparing meals.*

fabric should be put up to block the sky. Choose fabrics that are easy to clean and ensure that they do not hang too low and are not highly flammable. The same conditions apply to conservatory kitchens as to conventional ones. If working with the door behind you, place a sheet of metal or a large shiny object so that you can see anyone entering the room.

THE CONSERVATORY DINING ROOM

The conservatory dining room should be treated in the same way as a conventional diner, but there are difficulties. The conservatory room often opens directly into the kitchen and occasionally also into the main living area. There will be doors to the garden and two or three of the walls will be glass. This makes it very difficult to sit with support from behind, so it is important that chairs have high backs, and preferably arms, to provide this.

Depending on the aspect, the evening sun may cause glare so protective measures, such as blinds, should be available. Conservatories can be very warm until quite late in the evening and fans can help to move the air around.

Any water features in the conservatory are not conducive to good digestion and should be turned off during meals.

THE CONSERVATORY LIVING ROOM

Whether it is used as a living room or simply for enjoying an apéritif at the end of a long day, the conservatory will be a tranquil spot so long as adequate shade and ventilation are provided.

A water feature will cool the air and be soothing, providing it is placed in an auspicious spot according to the Five

◀ *What a healthy way to dine – absorbing energy from the landscape as much as the food and company.*

▼ *Curtains are not really necessary when you have a wonderful view like this.*

▲ *A wide variety of different foliage plants adds interest to this small conservatory area.*

Elements. North is auspicious as it is the Water position. If the conservatory sits in the east or south-west, then this is the spot for a water feature, which will symbolize present and future prosperity.

BALCONIES AND WINDOW-BOXES

Many apartments have balconies which are purely cosmetic and act as barriers between neighbouring apartments when the doors are opened. Others are larger but do not really enable outdoor living as such, having no room for tables and seating. Some apartments have neither but may have an external windowsill on which to put plants or window-boxes. All these small spaces bring the natural world inside our homes.

The outlook in many urban apartments is bleak. The most auspicious sites overlook a park or a river, but most overlook a busy road or even a brick wall.

▶ *Flowers in a window-box are guaranteed to lift the spirits.*

▼ *Even in a small space there is usually room for a windowsill display.*

CASE STUDY

A flower-lover who lived on the seventh floor was so troubled by pigeons nibbling his plants that he decided to give up trying to grow them. Yet his balcony still looked wonderful from below. He had purchased lots of green silk plants and ivy strands, and a collection of flowers to represent the seasons. Set in oasis and weighted with gravel, these saw him through several years and few people could tell the difference.

▶ *Silk plants are very effective in awkward sites and don't need watering.*

A kitchen windowsill, inside or outside, is a useful place to have a herb collection and bring not only the sight of the natural world into your home but also the smell and the taste.

The window box on the far left contains nasturtiums, pansies and marigolds, all of which are edible and can be used for flavour and garnishes. The window box in the picture on the near left contains chervil, coriander, fennel, garlic, purple sage, French tarragon, savory, oregano and basil – an entire herb garden in a box.

Many apartments overlook the windows of other apartments and we can be overlooked by dozens of eyes as we wash up or stand on our balconies. The Four Animals formation suggests that we need to define our space. By placing a window-box on our windowsill we not only define the Phoenix position, we also fill our homes with the Wood energy of growing plants. Recent studies have shown that hospital patients who overlook a garden recover more quickly than patients who do not have such a view. A healthy display of green plants to greet us in the morning will spur us on for the day ahead and welcome us home in the evening.

Growing plants on a balcony can be problematic. Compost (soil mix) is heavy and can be difficult to transport to the

▲ *This green oasis in a bustling city is shaded by an awning which, with the well-maintained plants, creates a protected space.*

◄ *Even a small outdoor space such as this will provide plenty of energy.*

apartment and also to dispose of later. Cosmetic balconies may not be able to cope with heavy weights and we must be mindful of this when choosing containers and plants. Bulbs can be a useful solution since they require a comparatively small amount of compost. A succession of bulbs throughout the year

will connect us to the seasons, which is auspicious in Feng Shui. Providing we keep them watered until the foliage has died down, we can lift the bulbs and store them for the following year. Depending on the direction in which the balcony faces, the colours of the bulbs may be chosen to correspond to the direction or to focus on a life aspiration, using the Bagua. Of course this is not essential; other plants may be used. It is preferable to plant shrubs and miniature trees and to use annual plants as spots of colour, rather than attempting to uproot plants and dispose of them several times a year.

SWIMMING POOLS

Large volumes of water exude power-ful energies and great care should be taken in siting pools with regard to the effect they will have on the area and the house, and on the elemental cycle of the location.

Large areas of still water are yin and in theory accumulate chi to balance the yang energy of the home. Where they are situated too close to the house, they can deplete the yang energy and cause problems. Auspicious shapes are those

▲ *This swimming pool is the correct size for the house and the points are hidden by the large bushy plants.*

with rounded edges and kidney-shaped pools which appear to hug the house.

POOL SHAPES

This kidney-shaped pool has no harmful points. It appears to hug the house and its shape is auspicious.

The corners of this L-shaped pool are sending "poison arrows" at the house and the swimmers.

Without the planting to obscure part of its view from the house, the energy of this pool would be overwhelming.

▲ *The flowing, natural lines of this swimming pool are in harmony with the surrounding garden.*

Where straight-sided pools are at an angle to the house, the edges of the pool can send "poison arrows" of chi to the detriment of the inhabitants.

Although a body of water in theory accumulates chi, there are other factors to be taken into consideration. The surrounding landscape, symbolically the Dragon, may have been excavated to create the pool and will probably have been damaged, or the appearance and energy of the place may have been damaged.

▲ *Here large rocks add stability to this lovely pool, while the vegetation brings life and vitality.*

▼ *Flowing curves and gentle planting make this swimming pool very inviting. The entrance to the house is well-balanced.*

Another factor is the direction of the swimming pool. A large body of water in the south will destroy the Fire energy there. The east and south-east are good locations since the water will feed growth and at the same time its energy will be kept under control by the Wood.

The colour of the pool tiles is important and care should be taken to retain a balance of the elements in and around the pool. Pale blue is a favourite colour, but again will not suit all locations. Refer back to "The Relationships of the Five Elements" table to ensure a balance has been maintained.

The size of the pool must be in proportion to the house and the surrounding landscape. An enormous pool in a small back garden can symbolically "drown" the occupants. Consider also the direction of the sun at various times of the day when you are choosing a site.

INDOOR POOLS

These are not recommended in Feng Shui and need to be well secured if they are part of the house. If you already have one, it should be kept separate from the house by closed doors. Pools in basements are considered a destabilizing influence, and rooftop pools are thought to symbolically "drown" residents and weigh them down.

THE HOME OFFICE

Home offices differ from studies in that they are more yang because they have more contact with the outside world. For this reason, they are better placed close to the entrance so that work does not impinge on the whole house and visitors do not have to walk through the living accommodation. Home offices can be difficult places, particularly when situated in the main body of the house. There is always a temptation to take time out to do household tasks, or for the family to drop in. Although home working allows flexibility, it demands a high level of self-discipline in order to work for long enough but not too long, to

▼ *A garden studio or office, removed from the main house, is an excellent idea.*

▲ *This luxurious office space is obviously designed for meetings with clients.*

▶ *If the chair and desk positions in this study were to be reversed it would open up a view of the outside world.*

allow time for social activities. A balance has to be maintained. Ideally, home offices should be placed where visitors have access via a separate door and apart from the main house, in a wing or even in a separate building in the garden.

OFFICE POSITION
The ideal position for the office is in your best direction or in one of the other three favoured positions. The south-west is not favoured for office locations since the energy levels are falling there. Wherever it is situated, some care in the north will be advantageous.

Any "poison arrows" should be deflected or hidden, using mirrors or screens. Metal supports Water so hollow metal wind chimes or a metal object would be helpful. Water is also auspicious here but do not use the area to display plants as they will drain the energy.

DESK POSITIONS
Desk locations are the same as those for the study but if there is a secretary or another person working in the home office the desks should not face each other. The secretary should sit nearer to the door to protect the employer from having to deal with mundane matters. Both desks should have the support of a wall behind and both should have suitably supportive chairs which follow the favourable Four Animals formation. If a desk is close to a door, a plant on the edge will protect the occupant from unfavourable chi.

When visiting clients are received in the office, the owner's chair should always be backed by the wall facing the door and the clients should be seated in the

THE BAGUA AND DESKS

Use the Bagua to arrange your desk according to Feng Shui principles.

1. This represents Career or the start of the day and should be clear to open up possibilities for the day ahead.

2. The Relationships area is suitable for brochures and details of people with whom you will come into contact in the course of your present project.

3. A plant here in the Elders area will help to freshen the air and symbolize longevity and stability.

4. Accounts and paying-in books should be placed here in the Wealth area, but not cheque books, which represent money going out.

5. Use this central area for the task in hand and then clear it away. Do not leave things to pile up here.

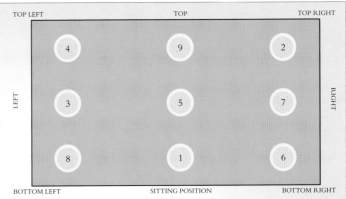

TOP LEFT · TOP · TOP RIGHT
LEFT · RIGHT
BOTTOM LEFT · SITTING POSITION · BOTTOM RIGHT

4 · 9 · 2
3 · 5 · 7
8 · 1 · 6

6. The Helpful People area is the place for the telephone and address book.

7. The Children or Projects position is ideal for putting the current project files.

8. Knowledge and Wisdom – the place to store reference books.

9. The Fame area and the Phoenix position. A crystal paperweight here will denote the boundary of your desk, and of the current project. An uplifting image or landscape hung on the wall in front will represent future possibilities.

▲ *This studio's view would be improved if the foliage outside wasn't so dense.*

subordinate position in a smaller chair, with their backs to the door.

Having sorted out the best location for the furniture, focus on the contents of the desk, either using compass directions or symbolically. Take care that any measures taken are not in conflict with the element of the area. Task lighting should always be diagonally opposite the writing hand to prevent shadows.

THE OFFICE ENVIRONMENT

Be aware of the approach to the office from outside and check for dustbins and other obstacles, overhanging branches and anything which will detract from your entrance. Inside the house, the same attention is necessary. Clients who come to visit you will not want to clamber over toys or other paraphernalia, which present an unprofessional approach.

It is important, particularly when the office is a section of a room that is used at other times for another purpose, to mark the boundaries – by a screen, piece of furniture or even a rug. Inside the space, aspirational images, landscapes,

▼ *This uncluttered desk is arranged following Feng Shui principles.*

FINANCIAL TIP

Tie three Chinese coins together with red thread or ribbon and place them in the back of your accounts book for good luck.

good lighting and bright colours all make a psychological contribution to success.

A clutter-free office environment is essential and work spaces should be clear of everything but the task in hand. Do not have stacked filing trays which, symbolically and literally, allow the work to mount up. Deal with letters and telephone calls the same day and note conversations and dates meticulously. Discard catalogues as new ones arrive as well as all out-of-date paperwork.

HOME STUDY OR STUDIO

The home study may be used by one or more members of the family to study for school or college examinations, for continuing education later in life or for pursuing a hobby or interest. It should be situated in a quiet part of the home, if possible. If study areas form part of another room – the bedroom, sitting room or even the kitchen – care should be taken to ensure that the activities of the two areas are kept quite separate, for example, by screening. It is not a good idea to use a bedroom as a home study, because it will no longer be a place to relax in.

▶ *Screens can be used to conceal work equipment in bedrooms and living rooms.*

DESK LOCATIONS

The three desk positions below have the support of a wall. You can also see the door and anyone entering. The desk on the right is directly opposite the door. The three desks below right are vulnerable from behind and anyone working in these positions would feel nervous.

Good: facing the door

Good: diagonally opposite the door

Bad: back to the door

Good: with a view of the door

Bad: facing a window

Good: here you can see who is entering

Bad: back to a window

DESK POSITIONS

The position of the desk is crucial if maximum benefits are to be gained from studying and it should be placed to avoid any areas of damaging chi.

The view from a study window should be pleasant but not detract from work. A view of the neighbours' swimming pool and barbecue area will not be conducive to work. Sitting opposite the windows of a neighbouring house is not recommended since it can cause discomfort, as can facing telephone wires or having roof points aimed at the office. If

▼ *An ideal solution – the folding doors allow light and air in during the day, and you can close down the office at night.*

there are distractions outside, the window should be covered by muslin, or something similar, to admit light but keep distractions out. Plants placed on the windowsill might serve the same purpose. Studies should have a good supply of fresh air in order to prevent tiredness.

When a considerable amount of time is spent in one position, the furniture should be ergonomically correct. Chairs should fit comfortably under desks and the seat should be at the correct height for writing and using a keyboard. If a conventional computer is used, it should be placed as far away as possible from the chair to reduce the radiation from the screen. Where possible, use a laptop computer. Trailing wires are dangerous and cause irritation, so tie them together

CLUTTER IN THE STUDY
Piles of used paper
Piles of unread journals
Out-of-date books
Cluttered hard drive
Noticeboards with out-of-date information
More than two adhesive notes
Broken equipment
Run-down batteries

▲ *It would be difficult to work in this room. The stacked bookshelves are also reflected in the mirror and are overwhelming.*

◀ *A Mayan chime ball hung in the window deflects the "poison arrow" created by the roof of one of the buildings outside.*

and tape them out of the way. Printers should be positioned to ensure the paper can eject easily. Plants in the study help to improve the air quality and also add some yin balance to the yang machines.

ORDER IN THE STUDY
The study should be as streamlined as possible and there should be a place for everything. Cupboards, shelves and bookcases will keep books and equipment off the desk surface. Coloured files and filing boxes store information and prevent paper mountains appearing on the desk and floor. Coloured adhesive bookmarkers avoid piles of open books and journals stacking up on the desk, but the marked items should be read in a day or two otherwise the stickers will be a constant reminder of things left undone.

Journals can pile up. You should try to read them immediately and discard them if they contain nothing of interest. If it is necessary to keep them, a small card index in subject order with the journal title, date, article title and page number will help you to quickly locate the items you want.

Once a piece of work has been completed and recognition received for it, it is unlikely that it will ever be referred to again. Consider whether a paper copy is really necessary. If not, store all completed work on floppy disks, which take up considerably less space. Remove past work from the computer hard drive to free up space and improve performance.

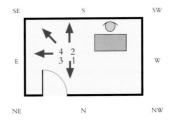

▲ *Ensure you face your best direction (or one of your other three favoured directions).*

PETS

F eng Shui is about environments and people and originally pets would not have played any part in the design of homes at all. Animals were domesticated as long as 8000 years ago but until quite recent times they were mainly used to work for their owners, and regarded as property rather than as best friends to human beings. Today, pets play a

▲▼ *Today pets – in particular cats and dogs – are an important part of a family unit and need to be considered in Feng Shui.*

very important role in the lives of their owners and their presence has to be taken into account when applying Feng Shui principles to the home

DOGS AND CATS

Whether we or our pets choose their sleeping places it is possible to ensure that the colour and pattern of their beds and bedding are in harmony with the elemental energy of the position. The table opposite shows the colours associated with each direction. Should a cat choose to sleep somewhere other than its basket, then there may be some geopathic stress which they are attracted to, or they may just enjoy snuggling up.

FROGS AND WEALTH

A china frog, carrying a coin in its mouth and placed inside the front door (particularly if it is the west or north-west, the Metal areas which signify money), supposedly attracts wealth to the house.

COLOUR OF BEDDING	
DIRECTION	COLOUR
East	Green
South-east	Green
South	Red
South-west	Yellow, brown
West	Grey
North-west	Grey
North	Blue/Black
North-east	Yellow, brown

PETS AND HEALTH

Although we get pleasure from our pets and studies have shown that stroking animals can actually relieve signs of stress, we should not be blind to the fact that they can cause health risks in the home. More than once clients have wondered why people do not stay long when they visit and the answer is so obvious. A litter tray in full view in the kitchen is the greatest turn-off for a guest, particularly when they have come to eat. Likewise, caged animals in children's bedrooms can create an unhealthy energy unless the cage is well maintained, and they are best located elsewhere. It might also be prudent to consider the health of the animals and we need to provide conditions which mirror their natural habitats and lifestyles as far as possible if our pets are to remain healthy. Just as human beings enjoy better health with good food and exercise, so pets will remain healthier if they are not imprisoned in confined spaces and fed on poor diets for the duration of their lives. The mental health of our animals is also important and problems often occur where pets are locked in a house or flat alone all day and often through the evening as well.

FISH

Fish symbolize success and wealth in China and an aquarium by the entrance or in the sitting room is thought to encourage this. Eight gold fish and one black one in a tank are believed to be an auspicious combination. When fish die it is not regarded as a sad occasion since it is thought that they are absorbing the bad luck of the family and the fish are replaced immediately. In the West, where animal welfare issues are considered, unless the tank can be large enough to provide a reasonable environment for the fish, a picture or image may be more acceptable. An indoor water feature in the south-east will serve as well. Outdoor pools, provided they are large enough and well maintained, provide a more natural environment. When in a front garden place them to the left of the front door, never to the right.

ANIMALS AND SYMBOLOGY

The use of animals as luck symbols is widespread in China and their symbolism lies deep within the culture of the country and does not necessarily translate into other cultures with their own symbols. Where a symbolic quality is desired, an ornament or picture will suffice to invoke the desired energy to an area.

▲ *Fish are considered to be very auspicious in China where they are kept to attract wealth to the household.*

▼ *An alert, intelligent dog such as this collie makes an ideal family pet.*

SYMBOLIC CHINESE ANIMALS	
Bat	luck
Bear	protection
Crane	health and longevity
Deer	luck and wealth
Elephant	wisdom
Fish	success
Horse	recognition
Leopard	protection
Lion	authority and protection
Stork	longevity
Tortoise	longevity

▼ *Animals need healthy diets as well as humans and our pets will be happier if they are fed regular, balanced meals.*

PICTURE ACKNOWLEDGEMENTS

The publishers would like to thank the following picture libraries for the use of their pictures.
Abode UK: 101br; 108t; 109tl. A-Z Botanical Collection ltd.:41br(Mike Vardy); Bruce Coleman: 125m(Werner Layer);The Garden Picture Library: 41bl(Morley Read);Robert Harding Picture Library: 105tl(IPC Magazines); 107tl(IPC Magazines); 108b(IPD Magazines); 109bl(IPC Magazines);Houses and Interiors: 40tr(Roger Brooks); 48bl(Roger Brooks), tr(Roger Brooks); 52tr(Mark Bolton); 53bl(Mark Bolton); 56tr(Roger Brooks); 85l(Verne); 88bl(Mark Bolton); 90tr; 114tr(Mark Bolton), bl(Mark Bolton);Hutchinson Library: 8br(Robert Francis); 10tr(Merilyn Thorold); 13tr(Melanie Friend); 26bl(T. Moser), br(Lesley Nelson); 27tl(F. Horner); 28t(Edward Parker), bl (Sarah Errington), r(John G Egan); 29bl(Tony Souter); 34tr(Pern.), r(P. W.

Rippon), bl(Robert Francis); 35tl(Tony Souter), bl(Carlos Freire), tr(G. Griffiths- Jones); 42t; 43tl (Phillip Wolmuth), t(L. Taylor), t, m, br(Andrew Sole); 68b(Sarah Murray); 69tl(Lesley Nelson); 71t(N. Durrell McKenna); 120bl(Nancy Durrell);Images Colour Library:; 11b; 12b; 13bl, bl; 14tr; 15no. 2, no. 5; 25br; 29tr; The Interior Archive: 1m; 8tl(Schulenburg); 9tr(Schulenburg); 44tr(Schulenburg); 48r(C. Simon Sykes); 54bl(Schulenburg); 55t(Schulenburg); 67tr (Henry Wilson); 74 (Schulenburg); 76tr(Schulenburg); 77tl (Schulenburg); 80bl(Schulenburg), t(Simon Upton); 84bl (Schulenburg), 86b(Schulenburg), 87tr (Schulenburg); 89bl(Schulenburg); 90br(Henry Wilson); 92t(Tim Beddow); 94bl(Schulenburg); 97r (Schulenburg); 100tr(Schulenburg),b(Schulenburg); 102l (Schulenburg);105tr(Schulenburg);106bl (Schulenburg);

110tr(Henry Wilson), bl(Schulenburg); 111bl(Schulenburg), br(Schulenburg); 113tl (Schulenburg), br(Schulenburg); 119tl; 122br (Schulenburg); 123tr(Schulenburg);The Stock Market: 14br; 15no. 1(K. Biggs); 36tr, bl, br; 37b, t; 38tl, m; 39tl; 64t(David Lawrence); 66br; 67tl, tr; 68t; 115b; Tony Stone: 66bl(Angus M. Mackillop);Jessica Strang: 120r; 123bl; Superstock: 22tr, m; 23br. View: 9m(Phillip Bier); 15no. 1(Dennis Gilbert); 43tr(Phillip Bier); 45l(Chris Gascoigne); 54tr(Phillip Bier), br(Phillip Bier); 55bl(Phillip Bier); 65tr(Peter Cook); 88tr(Phillip Bier); 94bl(Peter Cook); 96tr(Chris Gascoigne); 99tl(Phillip Bier); 115tl(PhillipBier); 120t(Chris Gascoigne); 121l(Peter Cook);Elizabeth Whiting Associates: 42m; 43m, tr; 44br; 48r; 60tr, bl; 61tr; 64bl; 69r, br; 70bl; 76bl, l; 77tr; 84t; 89t; 91tr; 93tl; 102br; 116tr; 117r, bl; 118t; 119tr, bl;

BIBLIOGRAPHY

FENG SHUI (GENERAL)

Lau, Theodora, *The Handbook of Chinese Horoscopes* (HarperCollins, London, 1979)

Man-Ho Kwok, Palmer, Martin & Ramsay, Jay, *The Tao Te Ching* (Element, London, 1997)

Ni, Hua-Ching, *The Book of Changes and the Unchanging Truth* (Seven Star Communications, Santa Monica, 1983)

Palmer, Martin, *The Elements of Taoism* (Element, Shaftesbury, 1991)

Palmer, Martin, *Yin and Yang* (Piatkus, London, 1997)

Walters, Derek, *Chinese Astrology* (Aquarian Press, London, 1992)

Walters, Derek, *The Feng Shui Handbook* (Aquarian Press, London, 1991)

Wong, Eva, *Feng Shui* (Shambhala, Boston, 1996)

UNDERSTANDING FENG SHUI

Franz, Marie-Louise von, *Time* (Thames and Hudson, London, 1978)

Jung, Carl, *Man and his Symbols* (Arkana, London, 1990)

Lawlor, Anthony, *The Temple in the House* (G.P. Putnam's Sons, New York, 1994)

Lawlor, Robert, *Sacred Geometry: Philosophy and Practice* (Thames and Hudson, London, 1982)

Lindqvist, Cecilia, *China: Empire of Living Symbols* (Massachusetts, Reading, 1991)

Mann, A.T., *Sacred Architecture* (Element, Shaftesbury, 1993)

Pennick, Nigel, *Earth Harmony: Places of Power, Holiness and Healing* (Capall Bann, Chieveley, 1997)

Poynder, Michael, *Pi in the Sky* (The Collins Press, Cork, 1997)

MODERN FENG SHUI

Cowan, David & Girdlestone, Rodney, *Safe as houses? Ill Health and Electro-Stress in the Home* (Gateway Books, Bath, 1996)

Myers, Norman (ed), *The Gaia Atlas of Planetary Management* (Gaia Book Ltd., London, 1994)

Pearson, David, *The New Natural House Book* (Conran Octopus, London, 1989)

Thurnell-Read, Jane, *Geopathic Stress* (Element, Shaftesbury, 1995)

GARDENS AND PLANTS

Flowerdew, Bob, *Complete Book of Companion Planting* (Kyle Cathie Ltd., London, 1993)

Hale, Gill, *The Feng Shui Garden* (Aurum Press, London, 1997)

Harper, Peter, *The Natural Garden Book* (Gaia Books, London, 1994)

Hu Dongchu, *The Way of the Virtuous, the Influence of Art and Philosophy on Chinese Garden Design* (New World Press, Beijing, 1991)

Huntington, Lucy, *Creating a Low Allergen Garden*

(Mitchell Beazley, London, 1998)

Liu Dun-zhen, *Chinese Classical Gardens of Suzhou* (McGraw Hill, Inc., New York, 1993)

Riotte, Louise, *Astrological Gardening* (Storey Communications Inc., Pownal, 1994)

Wolverton, B.C., *Eco-Friendly House Plants* (Weidenfeld & Nicolson, London, 1996)

Zhu Junzhen, *Chinese Landscape Gardening* (Foreign Languages Press, Beijing, 1992)

KI ASTROLOGY

Sandifer, Jon, *Feng Shui Astrology* (Piatkus, London, 1997)

Yoshikawa, *Takashi The Ki* (Rider, London, 1998)

SPACE CLEARING

Kingston, Karen, *Creating Sacred Space with Feng Shui* (Piatkus, London, 1996)

Linn, Denise, *Sacred Space* (Rider,

INDEX

NOTES

NOTES

NOTES

NOTES